Country Ways

A Country Year in Kent & Sussex

Also available:

Country Ways
A Country Year in Hampshire & Dorset

A Country Year
in Kent & Sussex

ANTHONY HOWARD

Countryside Books/TVS

Country Ways
is produced for TVS by
COUNTRYWIDE FILMS LTD.

First Published 1991
© Text Anthony Howard 1991

COUNTRYSIDE BOOKS
3 Catherine Road
Newbury, Berkshire

ISBN 1 85306 151 4

Front Cover Photograph by Oxford Scientific Films
Back Cover Photograph by Martin King (Swift Picture Library Ltd.)

Black and white photography by Tom Howard
with additional photography by Derek Budd (pp 6, 9, 12)

Line drawing by Pip Challenger

Colour Photographs:
Dennis Bright (Swift Picture Library Ltd.) p53
Derek Budd pp18, 71
Martin King (Swift Picture Library Ltd.) pp17, 36
Neil McIntyre (Swift Picture Library Ltd.) p72
Andy Williams pp35, 54

Produced through MRM Associates Ltd., Reading
Typeset by Acorn Bookwork, Salisbury
Printed in England by Borcombe Printers, Romsey

CONTENTS

Anthony Howard, the Executive Producer of *Country Ways*.

Night passes, and the white dawn is poured out over the dew from the folds in low clouds of infinitely modulated grey. Autumn is clearly hiding somewhere in the long warm alleys under the green and gold of the hops. The very colours of the oast houses seem to wait for certain harmonies with oaks in the meadows and beeches in the steep woods. The songs, too, are those of the drowsy yellow-hammer, of the robin moodily brooding in orchards yellow spotted and streaked, of the unseen wandering willow-wren singing sweetly but in a broken voice of a matter now forgotten, of the melancholy twit of the single bullfinch as he flies. The sudden lyric of the wren can stir no corresponding energy in the land which is bowed, still, comfortable, like a deep-uddered cow fastened to the milking-stall and munching grains. Soon will the milk and honey flow. The reaping-machine whirrs; the wheelwrights have mended the waggons' wheels and patched their sides; they stand outside their lodges.

Edward Thomas 1879–1917

INTRODUCTION

IT was blowing Force 3 or 4 when we set out from the beach at Hastings. It was a grey, winter morning. A dog watched us as the fishing boat slipped over the shingle and down into the surf, which was already beginning to pound the concrete piles at the harbour mouth. Flocks of gulls toured the sky, their cries drowned by the rising wind. The fish market was just finishing business after its early morning stint from 4–8a.m. A few fishermen and buyers leant on the rusty railings smoking and exchanging quiet insults. The tall, narrow fishermen's huts towered behind them. The boat, which we were there to film as it went through its routine of fishing, was a hundred yards ahead of us. We saw it lurch and buck as it hit the open sea and headed south-west along the coast. Then we passed through the entrance and hung onto anything that was solid as the waves hit us. It was going to be a job to stand upright, let alone to make a film. When we got out to the fishing grounds the wind was rising steadily. Both boats were riding high seas and this made filming as difficult as it can be. Certainly, it was going to be out of the question to switch boats at sea and to get the camera onto the one which was doing the fishing. We decided to do the best we could and then to head back to Hastings. As the great nets of fish and seaweed were winched onto the deck of the trawler, it was sometimes silhouetted high above us against the angry sky, sometimes deep in the trough below. Even the veteran fishermen on board were having to struggle to keep their feet. After half-an-hour we gave up and turned eastwards. That was when our engine gave up. Suddenly the diesel choked and was silent. We were left with the sound of the wind ripping through the rigging and the waves smashing against the hull. No skill of our skipper was able to get the shaft turning again. The other fishing boat was too heavily loaded with fish and with wet nets to be able to give us a tow. And we were swinging around like a broken kite on a string. The camera assistant had gone through his blue phase and was slowly turning a greyish purple. We decided at last to call out the lifeboat and we watched the maroons go up above the shoreline. Three hours after we had come to a halt our rescuers were alongside and had taken us in tow. The wind was up to force 5 or 6 by now and freshening towards a gale as we fought our way slowly back towards the safety of Hastings harbour. As we approached the shingle the problem was how to keep our bow straight on to the beach so that the man on the shore with the hook on the end of the winch cable could fix it onto the front of the boat and see us dragged safely up the bank. The lifeboat headed at full power towards where the surf was breaking. It cast us off when it was less than fifty yards offshore and made a tight turn to starboard, just avoiding grounding itself. We heaved slowly in but, at the last moment, a big wave turned us and we rolled sideways onto the beach. Men and equipment were shaken and soaked through but the man on the winch, with years of experience behind him, just managed to hook us on and we were dragged thankfully up onto dry land.

WE do not encounter such adventures every time that we shoot a film for 'Country Ways.' It would be very expensive if we did. But one thing all the films we make do give us is the chance to meet and to talk to the ordinary, extraordinary people who live and work in the countryside of Southern England and along its coast and rivers, on its farms and in its forests. They are the unsung heroes who contribute so much to the well-being of the English landscape. They know more about what is good for it and how to maintain it than all the committees of experts rolled into one.

IN a lifetime, the counties of Kent and Sussex, at one period two of the most treasured parts of the kingdom and most sought after by those in search of peace and beauty and tranquillity, have reached a point where it is fair to wonder whether any of their countryside will survive. The channel tunnel, and the railway and road links to it and to the continent beyond, may be responsible for finally destroying what remains of the good life in the deep south-east. Even the most stalwart of local people may not now be able to turn back the tide of traffic and destruction. One of the great ones was Tom Parker from Fareham, where he farmed a great swathe of the county. Often he used to ride his great bay horses across the border into neighbouring Sussex, where he had family living. And he was known from Kent through to Dorset as 'The Guv'nor,' a giant of a man with a strong will, a sharp mind and a great determination to bend life to the shape he wanted it. We made two of our films with him and he picked up the basics of our trade as quickly and as surely as he had picked up his great farming skills. One thing he could never understand though was why we sometimes had to do things several times so that we could get all the different camera angles on a scene. He drove a magnificent coach and four, with which he had won prizes at all the great shows in the land. One afternoon in the high summer we were working with him as he drove his coach round a beautiful circuit of lanes near his house. We had a camera in a helicopter as well as one on the ground and we needed to do this same route several times. The old man grew more and more exasperated as we fiddled about and tried to do our jobs. When I asked him to set out for the fifth time, he turned to me and said with his deepest growl, 'If I farmed like you make films, I'd have gone bust years ago.' It is just as well that the last circuit was shot from the helicopter or viewers would have seen the scowl on that normally sunny face.

Tom Parker had a fund of stories and memories from the good days before the south was threatened by overcrowding and human greed. He told his tales well with the sound of the Hampshire and Sussex borders in every word: 'A great ambition I had from the time I was seven was to make myself useful on the farm. Why I didn't get killed, I don't understand, 'cos I was always mixed up with these horses and, in those days, they were often running away. I remember being thrown off the top of the loads and hitting the ground, and people thought I was dead. And riding these cart colts for sport – just generally acting the fool – climbing trees higher than anybody else, and sometimes falling off and getting a thrashing from my old father. Never did me any harm that and more should do it these days. But my great ambition was also to make myself useful. So, as soon as they would let me, I used to want to go driving ploughs. But first I had to start by working the old donkey which we had – just to get the hang of the thing. Then I'd help out on the farm anywhere I could. After the donkey, there was an old horse turned out in the meadow those days. Half lame he was. I'd get 'im in and I'd go to work with 'im. And Saturdays I would go driving plough and make sure that the boy that was meant to be doing it would be given another job so that I could get my hands on the ropes. We drove three horses on the plough in those days. And there was plenty for a youngster to learn, I can tell you. Everything to do with the horses themselves and the plough, the harness, the state of the land and the weather too. If there was no ploughing or

Derek Budd, *Country Ways* cameraman on location.

carting, I'd go off rook-scaring or minding the cows. I'd always do something. I suppose I'm just the same now – over eighty as I am. I must be up and doing. I can't sit and look in the fire. I just can't. The busier I am, the happier I am. And that's how I was then. Didn't matter what the job was. If I saw a man thatching on my way to school I'd shout up to him, "let me have a go, George." I'd give the man a pint of beer, stolen from my old Guv'nor's cellar, to let me loose on the roof he was doing. It was a good way to learn the job too. And I'd listen to these old farm men telling their stories in the stables and the barns. Then when I had to go to school, I hated it. I just hated it. I couldn't make anything of it at all. That's why I've got a disadvantage. If I had been a good scholar, I reckon I should have got somewhere.'

In spite of this handicap, Tom Parker became the millionaire owner of thousands of acres of good, southern farmland. He was a big-hearted and generous man, tough as teak, but he also had a reputation for driving the hardest of hard bargains: 'I've often wondered about whether I've been ruthless. I can't think I've been too bad when I've got men been with me for fifty-five years. I can't believe that. We got two men with that length of service. They only come up Saturdays now to earn a bit of pocket-money. We got some thirty odd men been with us twenty-five year. And we got a lot of men, twenty or more, have been away and come back again. I can't believe that I've been too hard. I might have been with my own class in the dealings I've had with 'em, to get the best trade I could. But then I had to be. If I hadn't done I should have gone under. I suppose I was a bit like the man at the market when the farmer went to ask him the price of pigs and the auctioneer said to him, "Ah, do you want to buy 'em or do you want to sell 'em? Because, if you're going to buy 'em, they're very, very dear. But, if you're going to sell 'em, they're for nothing." I can't think that'd quite apply to me, though. Money's strange stuff all the same and the effect it has on people. To my way of thinking, it's no point to have money unless you make some use of it. There's a lot of people, you know, their only ambition is to die worth a fortune. I've known men that the first thing they did each day with the local paper was to study the deaths column to see how much other people had left. And they wouldn't give any away, these chaps, because they wanted to have it said that they died worth a big lot of money. Now, here's a bloomin' funny thing. One particular case it was of a man who farmed twelve hundred acres. He lent his son three or four thousand pounds to take a farm of his own, though I don't think he was very keen to loan him the cash. A few years later the son went over to see the old man and said, "Father, I could take another farm now, which is to be let next door. Do you think I ought to do it?" The father told him, "If you can afford to take another farm, you can afford to pay me back my three thousand pounds," And he made him pay back what he owed. Now that old farmer died worth a lot of money. And the funny thing about it is that his son is repeating it all over again with his children.'

The Guv'nor had risen from the bottom to the top in his lifetime. But he never seemed to forget about his early years and the roots from which he had come. Certainly he was feared. But he was also loved by many and respected by all: 'When I started out, farming was a very hard living. Mind you, I've often wondered whether it was worse than anyone else's. Money was very scarce. If a ha'penny could be saved, it was saved. And we used to talk about how we were going to save it. To give you an idea of the economics of those times, I knew one old farmer, who had quite a bit of land. Well, just before the War, he brought a pair of boot laces, and the tag came off. So he took them back to the shop the next morning to know whether he could have the lace replaced or a new tag put on. And that was the general atmosphere of farming. They killed their own pigs, baked their own bread, churned their butter and made their cheese, all on a very economical basis. Nobody had any money to spare. On my father's farm, the men's wages were twelve shillings a week, thirteen shillings for the more skilled labourer and fourteen for the shepherd and the ploughman. They didn't get any overtime, though they worked long days. They got a tip of half-a-crown at Michaelmas, according to the rate. And the shepherds had the lambing money, which would be three or four pounds once a year. And that's all the money they had. When they eventually got overtime, they only had threepence an hour. I remember my father employing men in the spring of the year, weeding the corn by hand. We weeded all the corn those days. Then, when evening came, we'd turn the horses out to grass after they'd come home from ploughing. At the end of the day, when he paid the men, my father gave them threepence an hour. One of them told him that the farmer down the road was paying four pence and that he'd go and work for him the next day. My father had to let him go because there was nowt left over to pay more with. Then, in my time, I've seen that whole thing change so that you wouldn't recognise it anymore. Those times the farmer and the farm workers were way down the ladder. The local doctor was top dog. He went round the villages in a horse and cart with a man that drove it for him. I knew the man well. He took him about with a good horse and trap with a cockade and a top hat. And he was a man who commanded a lot of respect. Just the same as the parson. He was another one people looked up to whether or not they went to church. But, you know, this thing has changed. To start with, I've seen the prestige of the farmers go from floor to the ceiling during my life. The farmer was looked down on, still hanging on from the days when we were all peasants. At our local church, in the front row, sat the parson's relations and family. Next sat the local squires, who owned all the land. There was three or four big houses about the place. They rented out their farms and cottages and lived off the proceeds as landlords. Next pew back came the doctor and then perhaps any military or professional people. Then, after all of them, came the farmers with the village blacksmith, the wheelwright, the undertaker and all the other tradesmen. Last of all were the farm workers and their families. And all the pews were allocated in that way. If you sat down in the wrong one, you were soon told to move into another. And that was how the thing went on.'

Those long lost days of innocence, poverty, hard grinding work and small rewards are gone forever. And a good thing too. But with them have gone much that is precious and valuable in the English countryside. Almost everyone is greedy and hard-eyed today and the land is the loser. Avarice crosses all class and wealth barriers and people have lost the instincts, which earlier generations possessed, to cherish the soil and to rest the fields and the pastures. Holidays in the sun and new motor cars have become more important than the well-being of the future inhabitants of the earth.

JACK Lewis from Balcombe, close to Ashdown Forest in Sussex, was of the same generation as Tom Parker. He was a gamekeeper all his life. If the cards had fallen differently, he too could have ended up as a rich man, for he had the same drive and determination as the Guv'nor. We went to film with Jack in all the seasons of the year, watching him as he coped with his work, his house and his magnificent garden,

Interviewer Jim Flegg looks on as Joe and Jim Pilcher shear one of their sheep on their farm at Creek End on Walland Marsh.

which occupied hours of his time and grew all the flowers and vegetables which the heart could desire. He had an unerring eye for the movement of animals and the growth of trees and plants. He would be the best of all friends and the worst of all enemies because there was no room for compromise in his life or in his thinking: 'If you've got some guts and determination, you can do almost anything. A young chap should never belittle himself. He's just as good as the next chap. He's better if he thinks he's better and shows he's better. I've never had no real education. Nor did my father. But he was a better educated man than me. I remember that he was the most marvellous writer. He educated himself and so did me mother. Today they get education thrown at them, and I know lots of young chaps as have been to various good schools and colleges and their writing is almost unreadable. And they can't converse either. They can't tell you what their troubles are. Their education's cost a lot of money, but it hasn't done a lot of good. Everything's too easy now. We don't have to work for anything. I remember poor boys at school – I mean really poor. Boys that never wore shoes and stockings. They went to school with nothing on their feet because they hadn't got anything. And their clothes were only cut-down pieces of cloth what somebody had thrown away. Now some of those boys were really outstanding and went on to good jobs – jobs of importance. They did well in military careers – in the army and the navy. Anything where there was competition they did well. And I think a lot of it was to do with that when I was a little boy, if you had anything, somebody took it off you. But, if you wanted to survive, you took good care they didn't take it off you. You stuck up for yourself. I learnt to do that and I'm pleased I did – and proud of it. As you get older I think everybody's thoughts go back and I've no doubt about it that, in everybody's life, some part of when they were young was the best time. I talked to a very prominent man – as a matter of fact he became Prime Minister later on – and I had a day with him out shooting. He talked to me at length of his boyhood days. He really enjoyed them. And so did I. And I think it's good to look back, whatever it's been, whether it was rough or smooth. Even if it's been very bad you think, "Well, I did well to weather that".'

Filming with Jack Lewis was always a joy. He was not patient by nature – not with human beings at any rate – but he learnt to be tolerant with the crew. The other pleasure was that you could not go through a day with the old man without learning something new. Wherever you went round his house and garden or in the surrounding farmland there were always animal tracks to be investigated, new plants to be examined, winds to be judged for the weather they would bring and smells to be savoured. He never lost the eager enthusiasm of his youth and his voice held all the excitement of a teenager's when he was on the trail of something which interested him: 'When something unusual happens, you can see it on the faces of the birds and the animals. The Chinese say that you can see it ahead of the event, which is supposed to be one way they can give warning of earthquakes. But, when it snows and there's ice on the ponds and lakes, there's a bewildered expression on them. They don't know what it is. You shouldn't be surprised either, 'cos with ducks and geese, instead of swimming on the water, they find themselves slipping about on the top of it. And that must be unexpected and puzzling. It takes days and days for them to get used to it. It affects them in several ways, but I think the main thing is that they take it for granted that they're far better sitting where they are than they would be worrying and looking for stuff to eat. I think they accept it and cope with it better in the end than we do. I can feed so many of 'em for so long. I don't think I can do any more. The majority of birds around here will come to where I am. I've not got to go and look for them. If they know there's a food supply, distance doesn't matter. If you clear a place in an acre of ground and put some food down they will come to it. They find a way to communicate and they will tell the others. Same thing goes for cattle and sheep. They're far sturdier than you would ever think. I was working on a farm one time years ago. I had some cattle, ten heifers and a bull, in a field. And it was terrible weather. I went out one morning and there were icicles on them. It had snowed and thawed and then it had frozen up again and the icicles were under their bellies – some of them a foot long. And I didn't know what to do to help them. So I made a shed out of tin and put some straw in it. But those cows never went in. They just wouldn't. The only time they used it was in the summertime to get out of the way of the flies. And they laid out on the open field in that terrible, terrible weather. And every morning they had those great daggers of ice on 'em'.

One of Jack's great skills was to carve and whittle sticks and to turn them into works of art. The small rooms of his cottage were full of stout walking-sticks with coloured handles – ducks and pheasants heads, badgers and foxes, cows and horses and owls. On winter evenings he would sit by his fire, his spectacles on his nose and a dead pheasant's head as a model on the arm of his chair, chipping away at the wood with a chisel, an old razor blade and pieces of broken glass. He could probably have sold the sticks for good money. But he never did. He either gave them away or he kept them: 'You want to cut your wood about Christmas time. It needs to be harvested, put in a shed and forgot about for at least a year. It's no good cutting it when it's green because the sap crinkles it and it's soft. You must take it in the winter time when the sap's down. That goes for hazel, ash and a bit of cherry if you like. But the holly, which makes some of the best sticks, that wants to be cut at the end of April or May, when its sap is down. And that applies to laurel and all the evergreens too'.

Jack would walk off down to the winter woods with the dogs scampering around him. The frost was on the growing corn and the sun was a deep red and low on the horizon. The old man looked sharply from side to side. When he saw something that seemed hopeful, he would plunge into the thicket. The dogs raced in after him expecting to find a rabbit or a pheasant. They looked disappointed when they discovered that their master was only after sticks again: 'You need a stick with a straight shank and a decent piece of wood growing out of the root or with a thick branch. The bit growing out wants to be as thick as your leg with a good, strong stick growing up from it about five feet long. The important thing is what is in your imagination when you pull it up. It's if you can see something in the stick. It may be that you've thought of a horse's head or a dog or a Harry Lauder stick. And then you try it and it's probably quite good.'

Working slowly and with no sudden movements for the camera, shooting in tight close up, the old cracked hands went about their delicate task gently and with infinite care and patience. The logs crackled in the grate. At last, the unmistakable shape of a pheasant's head began to emerge from the wood.

WITH the philosophy and attitudes of men like Jack Lewis and Tom Parker, the countryside of England is in good hands. At least, they are the hands which have carried it for a thousand years, sustained it and brought it to where it was at the beginning of this century. Only in relatively recent times have a mixture of the population explosion and the officious interference of people with little true love for the land and still less experience of it begun to threaten the centuries of effort which have been devoted to it. In an age of experts and bureaucrats we all seem condemned to have our lives influenced and our landscape blighted by their attempts to solve the insoluble. Far better, it seems to me, to leave the country in the hands of those who love it, whose families have nurtured it for centuries and who make their living on and from it. It is in their best interests to keep it in good heart for future generations. In the end, however much the politicians and the civil servants manoeuvre and manipulate, it will be the country people who will pay the price and who will bring the land back to where it should be.

THE LITTLE ROTHER

THERE are two river Rothers in Sussex and it is important not to get them mixed up. The eastern Rother rises at Rotherfield, swings over towards the Kent border and enters the English Channel below Winchelsea. To the north-west of the Walland Marsh the Rother Levels, bordered by the villages of Peasmarsh, Four Oaks and Northiam, enclose some of the finest countryside along the borders of Kent and Sussex. The western or Little Rother has its source in Hampshire on the slopes of Noah Hill below Selbourne and runs into Sussex past Rogate, Stedham, Midhurst and Fittleworth before joining the Arun at Hardham. Close to the south, the downs march along the side of the sea protecting this privileged countryside from storms and invaders. The old name for the Little Rother was the Scire, which means bright or clear. The western rivers of Sussex are more sparkling than the eastern ones according to Esther Meynell in her county book. And S. P. Mais, whose territory it was, wrote of this stretch of the South Country: 'It is England at her quietest and most beautiful. Everywhere there are poplars and oaks with tiny Church spires and towers peeping out from between the clustering trees, and ancient grey bridges at every bend.'

GEORGE Watson lives down wood and farm tracks high above Iping and the Rother Valley. To reach his cottage you have to open a gate in a meadow full of cattle and drive through the animals to the furthest corner, from where George enjoys views over to Goodwood on the South Downs. He came to the village when he was one year old and has worked in the countryside all his life. Now he has time to do some wood-turning and to make lovely plates, bowls and goblets. He is also an expert at tying fishing flies: 'The woodwork started when I met a man at a craft fair. I'd always been interested in trees and wood and I'd found some curious pieces locally. I showed them to him and, after talking for a while, I thought that I'd like to have a go at it when I retired. So I bought a lathe and started out. It's just progressed from there, beginning by doing simple, little things and then getting on to a bit more complicated. I find it very satisfying work to do. I buy some foreign wood, but in the main it comes from hereabouts. I'm lucky because I have access to quite a lot of the woodland round here. I find good pieces on the beach and birch trees. Mountain ash too is very nice to turn and there's plenty of that about. So I'm spoilt for home-grown material. There are people who think that only material from other countries is pretty. But they're wrong. There's lots of lovely wood in England. And that's what I'm looking for now to save me paying for the imported stuff.'

In his tiny shed George bends over the lathe. Showers of wood-shavings peel from the block and settle like feathers on the floor. The grain of the wood begins to add its graceful value to the bowl as it slowly takes shape. Outside, the snow of February still lies thick on the ground. Only newly dug molehills break up the white carpet. Icicles hang sharply from the gutters. The air is still too cold for them to have started dripping. A robin, fluffed up against the chill, boldly peeps through the half-open door, hoping that the falling wood chippings may be edible: 'This place suits me just about perfect. It's very cut off so, in the main, you don't see anybody you don't want to. Just the odd poacher from time to time. This part of the year there are problems of course with getting in and out, which can be quite exciting at times. In the Summer, of course, we've got everything. All the seasons have their compensations. You've got the garden and you can sit and smell the flowers and hear the birds singing. You couldn't wish to live in a better part of the country. We can see Butser Hill to the west and Chanctonbury Ring to the east. On race days, we're on the same level as Goodwood and we can see the sun glinting off the cars in the park there. You can almost enjoy race day without having to bother to go there.'

In a room the size of a big wardrobe at the far end of the shed where George does his wood-turning, the strong, stubby hands steadily wind thread round a tiny hook held in the teeth of a miniature vice. Nearby are brightly coloured feathers from native birds and from exotic jungle fowl. The smell of varnish is in the air and the eyes scarcely move as they watch every detail of the intricate work. On a shelf is a fine wooden case filled with fishing flies of every size, colour and description: 'This all began about 1960, I'd been fishing for years by then and I used to do a little bit of fly-tying from time to time. But usually I used to buy 'em. Well, I'd seen people doing their own in various places and, like with the wood, I thought I'd like to have a go at it too. So I started out and it just progressed from there to what I do now. I keep a lot of me friends 'appy and I've found a few friends that I might not have actually if I didn't tie 'em a few flies. It's satisfying work too you know. You've got something you can show people and which they admire. It gives them pleasure and, if they're any good, it catches them some fish too. It's quite difficult when you first start. Like most other things I suppose. A lot of people make the mistake as beginners of trying to do complicated ones. They're too ambitious. You've got to try something really simple first of all and then move on to the 'arder things. Nowadays, with the experience I've got, I can get some of 'em made in about three minutes. But if you get on to the more difficult ones, like the Irresistibles when you've got deer's hair which has to be shaved and clipped and all that, you're going to be looking for a few more minutes on each fly. Sometimes I come in here and sit down for a couple of hours and do a dozen, even a dozen and a half if I'm in the swing. Then I'll get up, stretch me arms and legs and go out for a walk round the woods.'

Close beside the centuries-old bridge at Stedham, George's solid figure is reflected in the waters of the stream. Here it makes a great pool round which early

'Heaven is free from clouds,
But of all colours seems to be,
Melted to one vast iris of the West,
Where the day joins the past Eternity.' *Lord Byron*

17

Royal coaches, Lord Mayor's carriages, wheels for wagons, spokes and shafts and old-fashioned skills and courtesy are all the property of Croford's in Ashford in the county of Kent. Wheelwright Nicholas Gill is one of their fine craftsmen.

bulbs are just beginning to push their way through the crisp covering of snow. Whenever he can, George, who has been a member of the Stedham Fishing Club since 1934, goes down to the Little Rother to try his luck on its slow waters: 'I've always enjoyed fishing the Rother. I've fished it for sixty years or so, so if I didn't enjoy it I'd be mad. It's a good fishing river even if it's not as good as it once was. I go to the Avon to fish sometimes and that's much more famous, but I still like the Rother. Fishing in February when it's cold like it is today, I shall probably have to settle for a grayling or two. I may be lucky and pick up a roach but its probably a little bit too cold for that. Once, when I was a boy about eight years old, a man caught a nine pound wild brown trout at Woolbeding. What a fish to catch. But I doubt there's enough water up there now even to cover a nine pounder. The real thing about fishing, though, is nothing to do with what you catch. It's about the enjoyment you get out of it. Because, when you sit by the river, you forget all the worries in life and the pressures that are on you. It's the most relaxed sport there is. You're by the water and, if you've got difficulties, you forget 'em. You're watching the float trot away down the river and everything but that goes out of your head. You can watch the wildlife and the birds around you. And I just wouldn't change it for anything.'

PETER Harknett has travelled the world as a steeplejack – a trade he learnt from his father. He specialises in church towers and spires and has made his home at Rogate, close to the Little Rother. From his house the view stretches away across grassy meadows to the South Downs. Often Peter has pieces in his workshop which were designed by Christopher Wren and other great architects of the past. He and his team make their own oak shingles and craft much of their lead work. But Peter really comes into his own swinging from a rope high above the southern country side: 'The weather-vane I'm working on at the moment is from the top of the spire of a Wren church in London. Most of the pieces are original and coated in twenty- three carat gold leaf. We took it down last week. We're going to repair it and then hoist it up there again. When we took it down we were more than a hundred feet above London, which, when they built the church, was an enormous height. In the old days from up there we used to be able to look down at the young ladies in the street and wave at them. Nowadays it's all changed. A hundred feet is nothing. You've got all those giant city blocks towering above you and the girls look down on you from their office windows. So it's been a complete change of geography in my lifetime. When we got up the top of this spire we assumed that the wooden ball inside the weather cock would be made of oak. But, when we took out a couple of the panels, we found it was made of chestnut, which is quite unusual for timber of this age. The wood is still in good shape and the whole piece would have lasted longer except for the War. The lead got damaged during the Blitz. They mended it after the fighting was over, but they didn't get it quite right. So now it's down again. Once we've got it covered with the new lead it will

Steeplejack Peter Harknett with one of the weathervanes he is so skilled at repairing and replacing on church spires.

probably last a couple of hundred years or more. And, of course, the old chunk of chestnut will stay as good as it is today, which is just right when it's an original piece of the church. I like to do things in the traditional way. I think they had it right many years ago when they used local materials. We manufacture our shingles out of oak and chestnut growing nearby. And I believe that we'll get a lot more life out of our building work than the people who have been using modern products in the last forty years or so. Recently we've been at work on Trotton church here in the Rother valley. It's a very picturesque and ancient building. It's got a perfect spire, which has been clad with oak shingles. We've just been taking them off 'cos they've had their life. And we've replaced them with chestnut. And what pleased me most is that the new shingles were cut on the hill beside the church. We worked in exactly the same way as the people who put on the oak shingles more than a hundred years before, except then it would probably have been done by the Estate workers.'

Close to the lovely old village of Stedham, Peter has a larger workshop where the shingles are made when it is not possible to do the job on site. The shed is filled with the sweet smell of sap and timber. The men split and trim the oblong, wooden 'slates' and stack them neatly along the walls: 'Oak shingles went out of fashion forty years ago because of the cost of the wood and the price of the labour to make them. We always made just a few for repairing patches on spires. But, after the great storm of 1987, oak has become much more available because so many trees came down. We can capitalise on that because we wouldn't want to have trees cut down specially. The chestnut we coppice, so that keeps on growing all the time and we're not doing any harm there. The skills that are needed to make the singles are not vast but it's hard work and slow and laborious too. A lot of man hours are needed because there's no machine can do the job. It's all done by hand as it always was. We once tried using machinery to speed up the process. But it didn't work. So we're now doing it as they used to a couple of centuries ago. The 'horses' that we sit on which hold the shingles firm while we work on them are really just primitive vices. They're traditional tools and they've been used nearly forever. The chaps who used to make chairs – chair bodgers they were called – used to have them up in the woods to hold the chair legs in place while they worked on them. We've tried using modern vices but the old way has proved to be the most efficient means of doing the job, which is rather a happy thought.'

From the top of the spire of Privett Church, a few miles to the west of Petersfield, you can comfortably see the Isle of Wight on a fine day. On a February morning, with a half-blizzard blowing, Peter and his team swing like spiders from the peak while the snow flakes swirl around them. The men move round the spire like moon-walkers leaning outwards on their ropes and pushing with both feet flat as they contact the stonework. A crazy staircase of ladders, some leaning backwards off the vertical, makes a dizzying ascent to the cross at the apex. This is no climb for faint hearts: 'What we're doing up this spire is a survey of the stone, which we'd normally undertake as a part of any steeple-jacking job, and also to try to stop the jackdaws going in. It's one of the biggest bunches of the birds I've ever seen. As the night draws on they swarm around, get inside onto the beams and make a right mess everywhere. In fact, down below, you're just walking through bird droppings. The only way to stop it happening is to seal it. We tried to do it from the inside and they got some other people to have a go as well. But we all failed. So the only way left now to do it properly is from the outside. People say that what we do looks dangerous and it probably is in a way. But it has its advantages. When you're up here you never get run over. You don't get anybody poking their nose in and talking to you, and you can sing as loud as you like and nobody complains. What more could you ask for than that? Another thing about it is that, according to the factory inspector, steeple-jacking is the safest job in the building industry. The reason is quite simple. You put your own stuff up and you work from it. Now, unless you're a bloody fool, you're not going to put up anything that's not safe because you're the one that gets into it. On a building site you get somebody else to put up the gear and they may think that it doesn't matter too much or that they can't be bothered. We use our own equipment, so it becomes a very safe job. One of the real pleasures of it is our contact with history. It's a great feeling to be the first person to revisit a place after perhaps hundreds of years. So when we finish a job, because we're so confident that our work's also going to last a long time, we leave a message at the top of the building. We put a lead envelope in the spire and seal it up, so that it's dark and airtight. That will be good for two or three hundred years. In there we put a record of what we've done to the church. We also sometimes find such messages from the distant past and you then can realise what those chaps were like, what they thought about, how they did their work and how much it cost. That last item has changed quite a lot, I can tell you. These records add to the church records, which are often quite sketchy and fill in all sorts of fascinating details.'

Peter Harknett's enthusiasm for his stomach-turning work is not in doubt. Variety he has in plenty. Each building he tackles is a new challenge and a new adventure. He says with a smile that, although he is Jewish, he has been asked to work on churches, cathedrals and mosques galore, but never yet on a synagogue: 'Once I was laddering Chichester Cathedral, which is somewhere about three hundred feet high. I got to the top of the spire and climbed over the cap. It's much bigger than you'd think up there. Two men can walk round on the top of it. Sitting up there was this kestrel watching us repairing the weather-vane. I don't know who thought who was the ugliest or who was the most frightened. But eventually he flew off, so I felt I won — even if he had had a much easier time getting up there and down than me. I don't always win though and specially not with the weather. Wind is the most unpleasant thing for a steeplejack. There's no conditions that you absolutely cannot work in. But, if it's blowing a gale and you're being pushed around by it, it's not very comfortable. It makes the work harder too of course. But there are always compensations. One of the beauties of being a steeplejack – other than the job satisfaction, which is the main thing – is that you get a view which pilots and birds enjoy. In fact, it's better than pilots because they're too high. It's a fantastic bird's-eye view of the world. You stand on top of the spire and look around. And we always take a photograph of the scene and give it to the vicar, because of course they never see this view of their village and their parish. And the countryside down here in the south is so special. I've lived in the Rother Valley for a lot of years and I've worked in the area for even longer. For me, it's the finest part of the country. You've got just about everything here – beautiful woods and hills, the downs, the river, old villages and churches. I don't really see how it could be much better.'

AT eighty-five George Ayling still cannot bring himself to stop work at the family nursery at Trotton. His grandfather was the village postman at Lodsworth and his father was a local gardener, who bought three acres of land in 1934 for £300. It took three men four years to pay off the loan. Even in the bleak and snowy month of February, George still finds plenty of jobs in the glass-houses to keep him clear of most mischief: 'It's cold enough outside today. That's for sure. But not as bad as we've had it in the past. We had thirty degrees of frost the other night but in 1947 we were down to thirty-four degrees of frost. And on one of the local farms it was thirty-six. I had a fellow working for me and he came along on his bike. I stopped him at the gate, called him in and said; "Brian, come and look at this thermometer. You'll never see it this low again." You could see the mercury pressing up against the steel it was that cold. That's the worst I've known it in my life. And that's been a fair old time. I left school when I was twelve in 1918 so I'm now in my seventy-third year of work. I still enjoy it, almost as much as when I first started. I'd certainly sooner be working than doing nothing. If the snow gets really bad for a couple of days I might not come over, but I'll always phone up in the morning to find out what the temperature is. I look on what I do as I imagine a doctor's job is. It's a profession. You can be taught a trade, but a profession you're learning more about all through your life. We've got customers that are doctors and we definitely have something in common. They're dealing with human life while we're coping with plant life – that's the only difference.'

The old man wheels a venerable wooden barrow between the rows of plants, which are growing healthily in the warm, moist atmosphere. Through the glass you can see snow falling lazily, the flakes melting as they hit the outside. As soon as the door is opened the icy air rushes in and bites at your face and hands: 'It started with my father, my brother and myself. It was three acres of bare land, pretty poor soil too and just rough grass. There wasn't anything on it. So we began by growing vegetables – brussel sprouts and carrots, parsnips, leeks, celery, lettuce, savoys and broccoli. Next we put up some little glass-houses on the other side and we used to grow tomatoes and cucumbers and all in there. Then in 1931 we took a shop in

Midhurst. We used to sell the produce there and then to supply the hotels and, later, the schools as well. We built up quite a big trade over the years and we used to sell a certain amount here as well as by the roadside. Well, we gave the shop up eight or nine years ago and now we sell everything from the nursery. So today it's plants, flowers, trees and shrubs because you've always got to grow the things you can sell. My son's always taken a great interest in shrubs. And I've always grown a lot of bedding plants – thousands and thousands of them. I used to sell them but we don't grow them any more now. We buy them in. But I still go on propagating the shrubs, as many as I can, and there are masses of them to do, which keeps me busy enough. The point about any plant is that it's a living thing. That's what makes it interesting. Money doesn't really come into it even though it's the way I earn my living. When I'm putting cuttings in I'm not thinking that they'll bring in this or that amount of cash. What I'm thinking is whether they're going to be comfortable and to flourish. I suppose I'm a bit of a philosopher really. I think the job does that to you.'

In spite of the month some of the greenhouses are full of colourful blooms and flowers. The smells inside are exotic and sweet, reviving memories of summer sun and distant lands. On an old bench George sits and painstakingly scrapes the names off a handful of old labels: 'I'll never throw a label away. I scrape them clean and use 'em again. I used to listen to a Professor at the London School of Economics and this is following his teaching about making ends meet. If you can use a plant label and then, when you've finished with it, you don't throw it away. You put it in a box or on a shelf and, when you've got a good bunch, you spend an hour or so scratching 'em clean and writing the new names on. If you use them three or four times each, it saves you buying new ones and that must be good business. That to me is making an economy. There's a world of difference between meanness and carefulness. You can be careful without being mean. And you can be mean without being careful. Same with holidays. People say I ought to take some time off. But I ask them who's going to look after my plants. They say that somebody else can do that. But then, if they're looking after my plants, they're not doing some other job which may be just as urgent. No one can do two jobs at the same time. So that's why I keep pulling my weight the way I do.'

TRACTORS are in the blood of Hill family. Ernie's grandfather drove one that was built in 1920 and would be worth a fortune if it was still around today. Ernie collects tractors and keeps them safely in his garden at the Forge in Ambersham near Midhurst. For his job he drives rather more modern monsters for the Cowdray Estate, where he has worked for the last thirty years. If Ernie was marooned on a desert island, he would definitely want to take a tractor with him: 'I suppose I was brought up with tractors and been in 'em all my life. I've just got one big craze for 'em. These frosty conditions are not so good for them with the ground hard where you want to plough, and ice and snow everywhere. But for

Ernie Hill with one of his collection of old tractors, though he uses the latest models in his work on the Cowdray Estate.

farm workers there's other work around that you still can do. We've got stumps to saw out, animals to feed, thawing out pipes and water troughs, machinery maintenance and hedging. There's plenty to keep us busy until the conditions come right to get us back on the land. But just to show you how reliable these forty year old Fordsons I've got still are, I started one up yesterday after three months standing idle and in all this freezing weather. Four winds of the crank handle and away she went. Then I just pushed the choke back and she was happy as she's ever been.'

Ernie is thickset, quiet and slow with steady eyes and well-worn hands. His old brick home has the bright yellow windows peculiar to all the farm workers' tied cottages on the Cowdray Estate. In the garden, snowdrops have survived the bitter cold and spring bulbs are pushing bravely through the white covering. Ernie, well wrapped against the elements, walks out past the beautifully cared for antique tractors. One of them is strap-linked to a circular saw with a blade more than two feet in diameter. The old engine roars into life, the belt engages and the saw begins to turn and to shimmer in the cold winter light. Ernie goes to work cutting points onto fence posts. The tractor protests as the blade bites into the wood, inside which the sap has been frozen solid. Bantams seem unafraid of the noise as they scratch and forage in a nearby hedge: 'I still have a yearning for these old tractors. I always love working with them. I'd sooner drive them than the new ones. The

25

only thing is that you can do more with the modern machines. What I surely don't want is a tractor with a computer on it. Some of the latest ones have 'em, even on this farm. But I don't want to move on to that. The one I normally drive has everything on it I need. And, to be honest, the old ones in the garden have all you want too — an engine, gearbox, hydraulics and something to pull. What good's a computer? It don't do anything for the crop. The one invention I do like is the radio in the cab. When you're stuck in there ploughing all day and you've got twenty acres and more to do, you're at it from seven in the morning until eight or nine at night, then the radio's a great help. I also think that the old way of cultivating the land was the best. Them days we used to really work it. Now, it's chemical sprays or your weed-killers and your artificial and the earth doesn't get nearly so good a chance. I think the old method was the way to get a good crop. Trouble is that took manpower and, like everywhere else, there's a lot less people here than there was when I first arrived. Everything went slower then and better too. Them old machines would only plough three or four acres a day. But they gave you time to enjoy your surroundings. In the springtime you'd hear the old birds singing and the cuckoo starting to come over and you knew that summer was on its way. And, in the autumn and winter, watching the seagulls and rooks coming in behind you. Them things all help to make the job a pleasure.'

SUSSEX woodland has produced hurdles, fences, posts and timber products of every kind through the centuries. Above Fittleworth, Albert Payne and his son Terry keep the tradition going in the nearby woods and in their busy timber yard. Here, the smell of the sawdust and the steady wood fire is as sweet as the scent of the leaves and the trees in the local coppices: 'This weather the chestnut gets frozen – right through. It don't clean as well. Also, the poles get covered in snow and ice. You have to knock it all off before you can work on 'em. So it slows the whole job down. Makes it twice as 'ard really. It's a tough enough way to carry on at the best of times. Start before seven. Finish after five. Every day of the week. I spend most of my time up in the woods — sunny weather anyway. When the day's really bad and wet then I come into the yard and help out. But you've got to keep the raw material coming in or there's no work to do. This is my world, my country. I was born within three hundred yards of the wood-yard and I've no plans to move now. The work comes naturally to me after all these years. I don't think about it too much any more. I just get on with it. I'm happy enough with what I've done and I wouldn't make any great changes if I had my life over again. It's been right for me.'

Up in the woods smoke drifts upwards from a fire fed by the debris of the chestnut coppicing. The snow still lies thick on the surrounding fields. The tall, young trees crash down as Terry wields his chain saw with practised skill. Within a few years healthy successors will have grown to replace them. Further down, Albert cuts the wood into lengths for the fencing which will be made in the yard. His measure is a gnarled stick, which looks as though it has been used for judging the length of fence- posts for decades: 'We're not just after chestnut, though that's the 'ardwood we use for the fences. We also take larch because that is made into panels for another job we do. We sell a lot of our stuff to the Council. You'll see it along road-sides or at shows. Gardeners use it too of course. It's all-purpose and all-weather. Good and strong too. After we've bought the coppice October-time and when the poles are cut and measured, it all gets brought down to the yard where it's peeled, clefted and wired up. It don't take long to say it. But it takes a bit longer to do the job. We've speeded things up lately though with a machine that we've thought about for a long time now. You've got to try and make life a bit easier if you can. It's hard enough as it is anyway. We used to wind the wire, which links the posts together, by hand. It was slow and grinding work. I suppose we'd done that for years and during that time we'd been having a good, hard think about it. Well, in the end we come up with the idea of a machine that would do the twisting and linking for us. We give the project to a chap who's a bit useful at making things and, after a while, he come up with what we use today. And it works a real treat. Lou works it while Terry and I cut the posts and get them ready for him. Terry, my son, has been interested in the job since he could hardly walk. He seems to have caught it from me. I remember the first day we went out in the woods together. I'd bought him an axe – a little one. The first swipe he took he missed the tree and he needed four or five stitches in his foot that day. Still, it never put him off and we've been together ever since. Business isn't bad so I think he'll be able to carry on well beyond my time.'

POUND Farm, Woolbeding near Midhurst, is where Martin Liverton and his wife, Jane, run their family business. Martin looks after the sheep and the farm buildings, many of which he has made himself. Jane runs a successful riding school, which makes daily use of the wooded tracks in the Rother Valley. This is perfect hacking country and the local youngsters queue up for rides: 'We're lucky up here because we've got so much common land to ride on, which means that we can do a minimum of road work. That was really one of the big reasons for setting up the riding school in the first place. It's such a marvellous area for the horses and for the children as well. Safety is so important. We also aren't too far from London, so we get people coming down from there as well. We've got great views over the Downs and over the other way as well towards Haslemere. We couldn't be more lucky really. Obviously it's not so good in this frost and snow because the ground's hard underneath. It makes it difficult to get the horses out at all. Then, when you do get them going, they're quite fresh and frisky. We've got nineteen animals in the stables. Eight of them live in all the time. They go out during the day when the ground's suitable. The rest stay out at night and come in during the day. Every-thing is harder work these winter months – water frozen, more food needed, harder getting about, thicker coats so the grooming takes longer, problems in keeping their rugs dry and so on and so on. It all makes you really look forward to the spring and summer when there's more riding to do and less problems to solve. Only trouble last summer was that it was so dry that the grass didn't grow very much. If you're not careful then the horses lose weight and condition. This winter we're going through even more food than usual trying to keep the weight on them and to stop them getting thin and skinny.'

In the barn Martin is surrounded by a mob of ewes and their tiny lambs, which sometimes almost vanish beneath a deep carpet of clean straw. Lambing is in full swing and the whole Liverton family is involved in making sure it all goes as smoothly as possible: 'We've got two hundred and forty ewes to have lambs and I can tell you that it's a lot better doing it indoors than out, like we used to. For one thing you can see. For another there's almost no danger from foxes and crows and certainly none from cold or wet weather. All right, the sheep may get softer and perhaps they're more prone to disease. But the pluses certainly outweigh the minuses. There's an example in the field today. By mistake one old ewe had her lamb over against the hedge before we'd brought her in. When I went out, there were two great crows standing over beside the lamb ready to peck at its eyes if the mother had given them half a chance. Well, you won't find any crows in the covered yard I can promise you, and it's a lot warmer in there too for the little blighters. The other thing is – and it may sound funny to some people – that the ewes are more confident if you get 'em in five or six weeks before lambing. They settle down, make themselves at home and get used to our way of working. To tell the truth, I reckon they sometimes feel a bit sad when we push 'em outside again once it's all over. It's hard work for us all this time of the year 'cos nine times out of ten they're going to start lambing in the evening time and they'll carry on till first light. But it's all worth it. There's nothing quite like helping to bring new life into the world. With all the problems there are in farming at the moment, it's tempting sometimes to think of doing something different but, once you've been brought up on an outside life, it would be an awful job to change it to another way. So I think I'll stay put.'

IT is hard to imagine that, in the last century, the lower part of the Little Rother was made navigable and that seven locks were built. There was barge traffic from Midhurst down to the Arun and then on to the sea. Coal was brought into mid-Sussex by water and Petworth marble exported by kindness of the tiny stream. Today, in the dark woods, the river still winds its way on its quiet journey. How comforting to think that what was once a commercial route is now a hidden place of serene beauty. Is it too much to hope that, in a hundred or so years from now, the same may be true of the sullen roads that rip their way through our precious landscape today?

CHARTHAM DOWNS

THE river Stour winds its way close to the south of Canterbury and divides just outside the village of Chartham. The two streams run through the village and for more than six hundred years have helped drive the mills which have produced paper of every kind and condition. Chartham became famous during the Second World War for manufacturing tracing paper, which was used by inventors and designers as they worked on their engines of terror. High above the village, Chartham Downs carry magnificent views north to Canterbury Cathedral and south across to the Garden of England and the Channel Ports. In spite of the surrounding tumult of what passes for civilisation in the back end of the twentieth century, these old hills remain remote and inaccessible. Tiny lanes wind their way through the chalkland and along the thickly wooded slopes. In the early spring the woods and meadows are just beginning to emerge from their winter drabness. The songs of the birds in the thickets are full of the hope of better times to come.

This is the place that W. B. Yeats might have been thinking of when he wrote in 'Where There is Nothing': 'As I can't leap from cloud to cloud, I want to wander from road to road. That little path there by the clipped hedge goes up to the high road. I want to go up that path and to walk along the high road, and so on and on and on, and to know all kinds of people. Did you ever think that the roads are the only things that are endless; that one can walk on and on, and never be stopped by a gate or a wall? They are the serpent of eternity. I wonder they have never been worshipped. What are the stars beside them? They never meet one another. The roads are the only things that are infinite. They are all endless.'

IN between the lanes on Chartham Downs some small farmers manage to make a hard living. These are not the barley barons of the Salisbury Plain or the dairy kings of Sussex and Hampshire. These are men who sweat for every pound they make and often have to struggle to survive. Gurney White and his three brothers farm a hundred and fifty acres at Crundale. Their family claims to have come over with the Normans from France nearly a thousand years ago. They can even trace their family name to a little village called Gournay across the Channel: 'Gurney is my first name and it's strange to think it's come down to me over all those years. I pick up traces of it from the wallet of an ancestor in 1795 and on a gravestone in Chilham churchyard. I think the family was in East Anglia for a time, but they've been down here for a century or two. My sixteen year old son has Gurney as his second name. He's not very happy with it. He prefers to be called Jack after his grandfather. One thing we all seem to agree on is the farming. It's not big or famous but we enjoy it because it's isolated. We're on our own and, on the whole, nobody interferes with us. It's a specially beautiful part of Kent which, fortunately for us, not a lot of people know about. It's eight miles from Canterbury, about the same from Ashford and two and a half miles from the A28. But when people get out here they ask, 'How on earth can you live in this place? It's so quiet.' And we've had Londoners here, who have gone away 'cos they couldn't stand the peace. Luckily though, that's the life we like. Family farms like this aren't that common any more. There's one or two still down on the Romney Marsh. Round this area though, there's only one other that I can think of. It's sad really because many of the farms are owned by people who've come from industry. That's how agriculture is going more and more with outsiders coming in. But it's not true farming as it used to be. Not like ours is now. We're four brothers with three of us here. The fourth can't do the job because he's allergic to animals. Mother still lives in the farmhouse and father died there five years ago. We've taken over from him and made do together. He came to this place about 1934. When he arrived the farm was derelict. The houses had a tree growing inside the main room and there was nothing here at all. He made it into what it is today and we're just trying to carry on in his footsteps. The future's up to us now to do the best we can with it.'

This is traditional sheep country. Hunt Street Farm has a hundred acres of arable land and about fifty of woodland and steep banks, which cannot be cultivated. Sheep graze in places where no tractor can go and where even cattle, heavy on their feet, cannot reach. Not so many years ago sheep would have spent the whole of the winter out of doors. Nowadays, even on such an old-fashioned farm they are brought under cover during the bad weather. In early March, with lambing just around the corner, they are getting proper VIP treatment: 'This time of the year I go through my morning routine with them every day. The ones inside get fed twice a day as they come up towards lambing. It's like human beings really. If you eat two meals a day you feel happier than eating one big one. The main reason they've been brought in is not so much the weather as the fact that we're short of grass. We stock them about five and a half ewes to the acre. To get the sheep out and healthy in the summertime you want as much grass as you can growing, and then as clean as you can have it. If we have 'em in a few weeks in the early spring that gives the grass the chance to get away and give them just what they need and want when we let them out again. Usually, we bring them in a month to a fortnight before lambing just to give the land a rest. Then, when they go back on the pasture, they're on grass they haven't been on for three or four months. The other thing about having them under cover in a yard is that it's a lot easier to handle them and to keep an eye on them. I have doubts about whether it's more economical to keep them in a closed area for such a long time. But when it comes down to going out to look them over at nights, they're just where you want them. You haven't got to walk all round the fields trying to find each individual or pulling them in out of the rain or snow. It makes life a lot easier and probably saves the lives of quite a few lambs too.'

Like almost every sheep farmer Gurney White has a collie to help him round up his flock. Working dogs, having a purpose in life, are more interesting than mere pets. They also seem more alert and less of a nuisance. If it is true that dogs are man's best friends, it is arguable that dogs which also do a useful job for their lords and masters, are priceless indeed: 'I've had this one called Gem for eighteen months. She came as a pup from a friend locally to take the place of our old dog, which was called Meg. We'd had her for nearly seventeen years and she was worth her weight in almost anything. Gem's coming along nicely now. She got her name because it's Meg spelt backwards. Whether the new one's going to be as good as the old, only time will tell. She's still got a lot to learn and, when I can find the time, I take her over to have some training with a sheepdog instructor. She's still young and that means she's fascinated by anything – particularly if it moves. She's too soft at the moment. I haven't been hard enough on her, but then you can't be too hard on an animal, can you? I'm too kind I suppose and I don't put in enough effort to train her properly. But she'll get there in the end in spite of me. She's got such a lot of heart.'

February has brought snow, ice and iron-hard frost to Chartham Downs. By March the thaw has begun and the White brothers are ready to start their early spring drilling. The corn is methodically sown, covered and rolled and, although the land is hilly and stony, the family manages to achieve good results by careful husbandry: 'I think my old father would be happy if he could see us today. He began it all and we've taken it on and carried it forward. He was here fifty years starting from scratch and he'd have felt, like I do, that to have your family carrying on after you is a beautiful thing. He might find some of the modern machinery and techniques difficult to understand. But you can't stop progress, can you? He'd certainly feel at home with brother Ian and his Large White pigs. He's got half-a-dozen or so of them and, after the postman's been in the morning, he goes out quite religiously and cleans them out, waters and feeds them. I go off and buy them for him every twelve weeks or so – and their food – and he does the rest. He keeps them spotless and does a truly marvellous job with them. Last lot he did got top prize as porkers and we were all very proud of him. Those sort of things make the job worthwhile. Anyway, this is all I wanted to do ever since I was a kid. Nothing else.'

To the south-east of Chartham Downs lies the Pett Valley. One of its villages carries the name of Pett Bottom, which has given much pleasure to humourists over the years. This is excellent horse country, and riding is popular with those who can afford it. That means work for farrier Fred Joiner from Willow Stud, Duckpit Lane, Petham, whose skills are in demand throughout east Kent: 'I always have to tell people that my job means looking after 'orses' feet *and* legs. A lot of folk think that a farrier just puts a band of metal on the bottom of an animal's hoof. That's not right. It's also to do with correcting all sorts of diseases and bone

Farrier, Fred Joiner of Petham, pictured here with one of his wife's Cleveland Bay horses.

ailments as well. Knowing about horses has to be in your blood I think. It goes back a long time with me. My grandfather was a wagoner. When we were children we used to go with him and his horses and that rubs off on you I suppose. The other thing is that we're surrounded by horses all the time and that's about all we talk about too. You learn something every time you do a job. The most satisfying part of it for me is when you get a horse with a deformed leg or foot. You work out what needs to be done, put specially built shoes on to correct the problem and get your reward when you see the horse going away sound and happy.'

Fred relishes his outdoor life and enjoys the wildlife, the woods and the flowers which surround him and his work. He carries with him sayings about wind and weather handed down from his grandfather. One that is particularly appropriate for the country of Chartham Downs and the Pett Valley reads, 'Mist in the hollow – fine weather to follow. Mist on the hill – water for the mill.' Another one, for his trade, says that farriers and blacksmiths do not retire. They simply die at the anvil. Fred's wife Pat carries on the family business in horses. She is one of the only breeders of Cleveland Bays in the South: 'She's a first-rate horsewoman too and she's done well with her Cleveland Bays up and down the country. Unfortunately they're becoming a rare breed now. We keep 'em going because they're a British horse and we're proud of that. So she runs a stud and I help her as much as I can with it, including the shoeing of course. I started doing that about fifty years ago. I was trained in the Army as a farrier. It wasn't in the family – my father worked in the hop gardens drying the hops and so on. But I joined up, went into the farrier shop and shod 'orses. I was in the services sixteen years, shoeing mules, horses and what have you in places as far afield as Greece and Abyssinia. One thing I discovered at that time was that mules are more sensible than 'orses, though it don't always make you popular to say so. Whereas a horse will lead you into trouble, a mule won't. He will stop before you get into difficulties. It doesn't help much round these parts though because there aren't no mules – the only ones we've got are some of the horse owners. Apart from them, the actual craft of shoeing is not as hard as some people think. They imagine that you need a lot of strength to do it. But you don't. It's much more of a knack really. That and you've got to have a way with horses as well. You gotta treat 'em like a woman. If they're good you give 'em a box of chocolates. If they're bad you give 'em a clout.'

To an outsider looking in a blacksmith's work looks hard, hot and painful. Technology has done little to help him except perhaps to provide a fan to keep his coals red-hot. The anvil has remained unchanged for a hundred years. Many of the tools are older still. And the forge itself, however picturesque, is still reminiscent of a Victorian sweatshop: 'Young farriers often seem to get bad backs. I think it's because they try to do two days work in one. In my opinion a man should only shoe five horses a day. These youngsters try to do ten or more and then they're surprised when something goes wrong with 'em. Being hurt by getting kicked you can't do so much about. It's part of the job I suppose. It's not too comfortable but it's better than being bitten. I really don't like that at all and I blame the owners to some extent 'cos I reckon it's up to them to stop them biting. You don't want that sort of interruption or upset when you're working with red-hot metal. I always hot shoe horses. I don't believe in making them in advance and then putting them on cold. There was an old saying told me by a farrier many years ago that 'cold-iron blacksmiths go to hell.' And the fact is that it's very difficult, if not impossible, to fit properly a shoe that isn't hot. With hot shoeing you go through the same procedure as cold shoeing. You take the old shoe off, level the foot as best you can and trim it. Some people think that, with a red-hot shoe, you burn into the hoof and make a seat for the shoe to sit in. But that's not it at all. All a hot shoe does when it touches the hoof is to show up the high spots and the low spots. You hold the shoe on for a little while and where it burns it's very high and where it doesn't burn it's low. So you rasp off the high spots and then gradually level the foot. The reason it's important to get this absolutely right is that the horse's feet have got to be balanced – as near perfect as possible. His tendons and his ligaments twist if he's not balanced properly. Each leg and each hoof is a pillar of support for the animal to balance on. If the base is wrong then the limb is wrong and that means the horse can be damaged and the rider injured. That's something you learn how to deal with over the years. It makes the job interesting and, in the end, you don't want to do anything else. When I was in the Army there was great comradeship with horses. They became part of your life. You can't get away from it because it's in your blood.'

THIS part of Kent is already feeling the influence of the Channel Tunnel. Once the hole under the sea is dug and trains are running through it the effect will be more dramatic still – some would say catastrophic. Ashford, once a sleepy market town, is now a motorised metropolis, surrounded by fast roads, modern housing and tired commuters. Pockets of resistance remain, however. One of them is at Croford's in the town centre. Here coaches from a long lost age are still built and repaired and wheelwrights practise their ancient skills. Clive Bampton is one of the craftsmen who started his working life as an apprentice here straight from school: 'One of the best things about Croford's is that it is a family business. We manage to work together very much as a family too. There are normally seventeen to twenty of us on the shop floor. Most people can, if needed, do most of the other jobs and we work well together as a small group. Our customers come from all walks of life. They might be local people who want a reproduction carriage or butchers who like to show off a traditional cart instead of the vans they might normally use. From there it goes right up to the Corporation of London or Buckingham Palace and Windsor Castle. Mainly people are wanting a restoration job done on an old vehicle. But we sometimes get a commission for a new one. Harrods, for instance, took two from us quite recently. Then we have a contract for the maintenance of the horse-drawn vehicles which are owned by the Corpora-

Old Scotney Castle on the Kent and Sussex borders and just to the south-east of Lamberhurst.

'It is a reverend thing to see an ancient castle or building not in decay'   *Francis Bacon*

The reed warbler has unwittingly bitten off more than it can chew with this vast and unwelcome cuckoo in its nest. Strange that, unlike human beings, birds seem willing to shrug and to put up with such a gross invasion – and to feed it relentlessly.

tion of London. We attend the Lord Mayor's Show every year, prepare the vehicles and attend it. So we have a solid and reliable market. Twenty years ago we were making about a thousand wooden wheels a year and they were almost all industrial wheels – for coster-barrows, handcarts, pony traps, and that type of thing. Now the emphasis has changed completely to private driving. But we're still building around a thousand wheels a year. So the market isn't increasing, but it's changed. Coach-building is pretty much in the same state. Now the competition vehicles have come onto the scene. We built the first two of them that were made in this country, but we don't make them anymore now. We made the decision not to get into that. But we supply wheels and components for the people who do specialise in that type of vehicle. Generally though our coach work is restorations – new shafts, repaired wheels, re-upholstered seats, a paint job all over and fresh tyres. They go out looking like new and that makes up ninety percent of our carriage work. We occasionally do gypsy caravans. We've been working on one here for eighteen months and it's nearly done now. The structural work is finished and we're soon going to start painting.'

The labour is intricate and painstaking. The smell of paint and varnish, wood and leather fills the workshop. This is a job for steady hands and experienced heads. Nothing is mass-produced or rushed. No detail is too small to ignore. Nothing second-rate is accepted: 'We're lucky to have such satisfying work to do. Somebody will start a job and, to a large extent, he's designing what he's making as he goes along. Although one wooden wheel looks pretty much the same as another, in actual fact they're not. There are real differences between types and designs. It's interesting because we can look at wooden wheels that have been made here in the past and, by the design of the hubs, we can tell who's worked on the wheel and which one of us built it in the first place. The materials we use are still traditional in the main. The timbers are elm for the hub, ash or oak for the spokes and elm or ash for the fellies, which are the sections making up the rim. The tyres can either be flat steel or rubber, depending on what they're going to be used for. We do sometimes build more modern wheels for competition work. They have aluminium flanges and they're designed to bolt onto small trailer hubs like mini car wheels. Our machinery, on the wheels side of the business, dates from the turn of the century. It's Victorian equipment and still works perfectly well. We get very few problems with it. The equipment was all originally powered by one engine in the British Wheel Works, which was here in Ashford. It used a system of countershafts and pulleys. But now, of course, each machine has an individual, electric motor. As far as the length of life of our wheels is concerned it obviously depends a lot on the conditions in which they operate. If it's being used somewhere with big temperature changes, you get a lot of expansion and contraction of the timber. Then the wheel will deteriorate far quicker. The same happens if there's too much moisture. In this part of southern England we would expect our wheels to last for at least fifty years if they're looked after properly. For instance they might require the occasional 'cut and shut' – that means removing the tyre, taking a slice out of it, tightening it slightly and resetting the joints. But the timber itself would last for half a century and we've had wheels in for repair which we know are ninety years old and have not been mended in the meantime.'

One encouraging factor for the future of Croford's is that all ages are represented on the team. When the oil under the desert has dried up or drained away, there will still be a nucleus of people who will be able to train others to build wheels and carriages for twenty-first century commuters as they trot along the M25: 'Most of our staff start straight from school. Very few leave, though some have gone away and then come back again. So I think they must enjoy the work in the main. It takes a certain type of person obviously – those who have a real pride in what they do. Most of the lads like to be connected to a job and to follow it through. Almost always, if somebody starts on something, he'll carry on with it to the end. So we don't have a production line in the sense that someone does a small part of a job and then hands it on. It means the men have to be versatile and flexible to be able to do most of the different things required on any one job. I doubt the business will expand much, but I can't imagine that it will ever die. There'll always be people who will want to use horses and to drive them in a traditional way.'

RIVER fishing is becoming a privileged sport in the south of England. Further north and west it is still possible to get your rod over the water with relative ease. In the South Country the amount of good water is on the decrease and the number of hopeful fishermen is booming. Trout lakes take up some of the slack but they hardly offer the same kind of experience as the Test or the Avon or the wild, white waters of Scotland and Wales. Charles Jardine has lived beside the Great Stour and close to Chartham Downs for more than thirty years. He caught his first fish there when he was three years old. In addition to fishing, Charles is a writer, artist and accomplished maker of fishing flies: 'I suppose it's unusual for a fisherman to paint. But I didn't have much choice really. I was born into a family of fishermen artists and, if I'd taken up golf, I don't suppose I'd have been easily forgiven. Anyway, it seems the most natural thing in the world to me to paint the life I see about me as I fish. They are things which I feel in my element with – fish, flowers, birds, water and so on. But I wouldn't dream of trying to paint steam-engines or cars. I just don't know enough about them. Sitting and becoming part of a river bank or a lakeside comes naturally to me – and so does the painting of them. One of the talents you have to learn is to memorise things. Wildlife has the irritating habit of not waiting for you while you paint it. So you have to take in something very quickly and then work on it from memory. It teaches you to be quiet too – angling also teaches you that. You've got to be an unobtrusive presence on the bank. You need to be at one with the countryside. You bury yourself in the undergrowth and, after a bit, birds and animals treat you as one of themselves. I don't suppose it's quite the same with flies and insects, which I also paint. But you need patience with them too.

I think perhaps photographs of them might be more satisfactory but I'm an artist, not a photographer, and so I think there's still a place for my pictures.'

Fishermen look at you as if you are mad if you suggest to them that their sport might be a little boring. Golfers have the same reaction. It is probably a human weakness to imagine that what entertains, interests and relaxes you must have the same effect on the rest of the human race. What is usually true is that the locations where fishermen choose to pass their time are the kind of places where even the most mean-spirited person will find visual pleasure and some mental peace: 'It's a mixture of so many things. But it would be wrong for anglers to think that they're on a higher plane than other human beings. When it comes down to the basic things we've none of us really changed very much since the Stone Age. There's an instinct in most people to hunt for food and it's a genuine urge inside you. Fishing and a lot of other country pursuits satisfy that primeval need. The curious thing about fly-fishing – and perhaps a sign that we are changing a little – is that by doing it in this way we're making it harder for ourselves to catch anything. We're putting up barriers between ourselves and the pursuit of our prey. It's by no means the most effective way of catching fish. I suppose that would be netting. I've even tickled trout, which I imagine is how the whole thing started. It's more difficult than using a rod and fly and I wouldn't advise anybody who wants to eat fish for supper to try it. The other strange thing about fly-fishing is the fly itself. When you look at a fishing fly as an attempt to imitate a living creature, it's ludicrous. The two things look nothing like one another. Yet I could sit down in front of my vice and fashion the most detailed insect. I'd put in every component and colour detail by detail. But that fly would not catch fish because it lacks the illusion of life. A fly-tier can build that illusion into his work even if his creation looks like nothing that lives. By choosing the right materials you get different effects. Black colours oddly enough seem to work throughout the year in varying places and at different depths. Dark tones also work better in cold water because the insect life is sombre. You don't have the brightness of summer or the warmth, and everything's a bit dowdy. One of the most important items you need when you're tying flies is the cape – the back feathers – of a chicken or a cockerel. A hen cape is softer. A cockerel cape tends to have more fibre. They're more spiky and more suitable for dry flies, which have to float. Nowadays, they're even breeding poultry specially for fly-tiers, though most of what we use comes from the food factories. I tie flies out of necessity. I lose too many on trees not to do so. When you've lost a fly you have to make another one to take its place in the box. You can't have an empty space in your fly box. That's the trouble with all fishermen. They tend to be magpies. If they haven't got something then they must get hold of it. They cram their boxes with scores of these amazing creations – very expensive some of them too – and then they probably only ever use about five.'

ONCE upon a time the North Downs of Kent were heavily wooded. This gave work to hundreds of foresters, hurdle-makers, charcoal-burners, gamekeepers

Trevor Austen devotes much of his time to carrying on the ancient craft of rake making for local farmers and gardeners.

and carpenters. Traces of these crafts remain. Today in a barn at Smeath, close to the Pilgrim's Way, Trevor Austen makes rakes for local farmers and gardeners. He does not start this job until the afternoon. Early every morning he is up before dawn on a milk round: 'The rake-making is a satisfying job. You can lose yourself in it. The smell of the wood gets into you too — not as much as a bonfire but in the same kind of way. The work is a good contrast to the milk round because it's doing something practical with my hands. Creating something out of wood is good for the soul, I reckon. You feel a lot more contented at the end of the day, though you can certainly feel frustrated when it goes wrong. My connection with wood comes from the fact that my father was a charcoal-burner. So we had access to the woods when we was children, specially me and my two eldest sisters. Then later I started work with four and a half years on a hop farm. Next I went to a fencing company for twelve months and began cutting wood and making stakes. I learnt a lot during that time. Later I took to making rakes and had a five or six year go at that until the trade all seemed to dry up. Anyway, the place I'm in now has been producing rakes for over a hundred years. Mostly hay-rakes and other long-handled ones. I've added one or two new lines and altered the design of some of 'em so they'd be a bit more appealing to the ladies. That meant cutting down the size of the head so it wasn't so bulky, shortening the handle and adding a few more teeth. It's used for leaves and working around the garden while the bigger ones are for farms and paddocks. At my peak I've been turning out ten or twelve dozen a week – probably even more. When I first began they only cost eight or nine shillings each.'

In the era of metal and plastic there is something reassuring about tools made from wood. There is also comfort in the knowledge that Trevor's rakes are identical to the ones which his predecessors were making a hundred years ago. The methods he uses to construct them are almost unchanged as well – even if the tools are more modern: 'We find an ash plantation twelve to fifteen years old and cut it in the winter. Often the wood isn't just as straight as we'd like it so we steam it so that it's all right to be used as a handle. You put the sticks in the steam for two or three hours depending on how much bend there is in them. It's trial and error really as to when you know they're ready. After the steaming we go through the whole process of making the rakes. It may all look a bit ramshackle, but it's not really. Years ago a group of businessmen came out here from Ashford to see how a production line was set up – one stage of work moving steadily on to the next. So we can't be that old-fashioned, can we? And the barn itself may seem a little tumble-down too. Experts came over and said it would fall down in a gale. Well, we've survived two hurricanes now and the buildings they told me were safe and sound – many of them disintegrated. I've learnt by now to do every job by myself. I can operate the saw-bench alone – in fact, I prefer it that way. When you're working on your own, you've got no one else to look out for. I enjoy the solitude and, in any case, my milk round more than makes up for any loneliness. I have to do that to pay the bills because there's just not enough money in making rakes. And I don't know how much longer I'm going to be able to keep it up. But the two jobs work well together. There's time in the twenty-four hours to fit both in and they're different enough to put some variety into my life. I'd like to think that I can go on like this for a while yet.'

KENT is a county torn by contradictions. On the one hand there is the Garden of England, the Downs and some magnificent, though shrinking, stretches of coastline. On the other there are the Channel Ports and Tunnel, the new roads and motorways and the building surge brought about by the county's closeness to London. These two opposing forces are unreconcilable. Nature, beauty, wildlife and tranquillity will always, in the short term, be conquered by man's greed and desire for speed, comfort and convenience. In the longer term there is perhaps some reason to hope that the weak may yet defeat the strong, the civilised the uncivilised, the simple the complicated. The time may still come when the countryside of old England, however badly exploited, can still return to its former glory.

LYMINGE FOREST

LYMINGE Forest is smaller than it was in its heyday. But it still spreads its shadow across hundreds of acres of Kent from Barham near Canterbury down to Stowting which sits between Ashford and Folkestone. Writing of this area in her book, 'The Bulwark Shore', Caroline Hillier described the beauty of the country which she so much admires: 'Inland from Dover is some of the loveliest country in Kent. . . . In spring it epitomises the misty, white ethereal quality of Kentish scenery, with tall hawthorn hedges and white pear blossom, sheep and streams, a tracery of branches against pale hillsides – a land in which the past is in the stones, the water and the trees.'

The great trees still dominate Lyminge Forest, even though many have crashed to their death in the storms of recent winters. Much of it now looks like scenes from the battlefields of the First World War. But Nature in her indomitable way continues to fight back. Birds and animals manage to thrive among the fallen giants. Flowers flourish in the newly created glades where the sun is now able to shine for the first time in decades. And young trees push their roots into the thin soil eager to replace the generation that has gone.

There are some evocative and ancient places in this unspoilt part of the far South-East. Mockbeggar, West Wood, Elham Park Wood and Parkwood make up the forest between Stelling Minnis and Stowting. Further north are Atchester Wood, Covert Woods and Gorsley and Charlton Woods. The names echo back through the centuries as do villages like Lynsore Bottom, Wheelbarrow Town, Rhodes Minnis, Lymbridge Green, Bladbean and Bossingham. Pines planted sixty years ago dominate Lyminge Forest but there is plenty of oak, beech and chestnut as well as the elegant silver birch, much loved by artists but much loathed by lovers of heathland onto which it greedily encroaches.

Some of the great views of Kent can be found here. The North Downs stride to the west of Lyminge Forest. The Elham Valley lies close to the east. Romney Marsh and the Channel are in the south and distant prospects of Canterbury Cathedral can be seen northwards. With a little patience and persistence much of the remaining beauty of Kent is within your grasp from this vantage point. Because of its height and the narrowness of the lanes which serve it, this is a pleasantly secluded and untroubled place. In the cold months of winter it is often cut off by snow and ice. The people who live here have, because of their comparative isolation, managed to hold onto most of their privacy and their independence in contrast to so much of the rest of the over-populated South-East.

'BROODY' Godden is a woodsman and has worked in Lyminge Forest for thirty-five years. His work has hardened him and made him fit, and he is now as much a part of the woodlands as the bracken and gorse and the trees themselves. He can fell a big fir tree, strip it of its branches and cut it into lengths in the same time as it would take most people to have a teabreak. He would no more want an indoor job than he would like to become a ballet dancer: 'I come from farming stock. My people and theirs before them worked on the land. The money wasn't all that good in agriculture in the fifties, so I thought I'd try a change. I came up here in 1957. Of course, everything was done by hand then – crosscut saws, bushman's saws and axes. There wasn't too many lifting machines to haul the cut wood out then either, so we did a lot of back work, carrying it all out to the nearest ride. Mechanisation has made the job a lot easier. In the early days we were mostly cutting pit-props for the Kent collieries. Quite small stuff really compared to what we do now. But there's none of that left because the collieries have all closed. The timber we handle has got bigger today because the machinery makes it possible. Chainsaws and lifting machines mean that we deal with pieces that you could never take on your back. At the same time you've still got to respect the modern things – just the same as you did in the old days. In the wrong hands anything we use in the woods can be dangerous. I've been lucky on the whole. I've cut myself more times with an axe than I want to think about – but never yet with a chainsaw. They wasn't small cuts either. One time I nearly had my foot off. Trouble with an axe is that, once you've swung it, if it happens to deflect on something, there's no stopping it. It's on it's way down and there's no chance of getting out of the way of it. Most modern machines has safety devices and guards. But however much the equipment has changed, the Forest has stayed pretty much the same. There's still lots of open air and I'm my own boss. Nobody's breathing down my neck. I always treat Lyminge Forest like it was my own garden, because this is where I started and this is where I've done most of my work.'

'Broody' is a big, bright-faced man with a halo of silver hair. He moves easily among the trees as he chooses the ones he is going to fell and decides how best the job can be done. Close by, giant tractors haul impossible loads of timber between the uprooted remains left by the hurricane: 'There's no other word for what's happened here than devastation. It's Nature at its most fierce. It's certainly made a lot of work for us but it's made it harder because it's easier for us to cut a tree down that's standing up straight than one that's gone over by the root. The trouble with the ones that are half blown over is that you can't get to the front of them. It's difficult to set them up properly and they split. It's strange to say but it takes longer to cut a tree down that's gone over by the root than it does one that's standing up. The other thing is that it's disturbed the whole rhythm of the job for us. Every five years we used to go round a plantation and thin it out. Now the wind has done all the woods and every age of tree in one go. January they were coming down round us while we were working. And that's a worry we don't usually have. It made the normal felling job seem quite simple. If you've got a big tree standing there ready for cutting, first of all you have a good look at it to see which way it's going to fall. Most times here they're going to drop away from the prevailing wind, which is from the west. So they'll almost always go from west to east. That is until you find one that's grown a bit funny. It's going to decide to drop the other way. So you have to have another look at that one, clear round the bottom, set it up and then away you go. There's a sadness in cutting them down. They take sixty years to grow and probably less than a minute to cut down. That makes you think a bit. But after all's said and done it's only a crop. So you've got to look at it as though it's harvest time. When so many years are up, it's time to cut and get the rewards for your patience. After we've been through the woods doing the cutting, all the brush and rubbish is cleared and burnt. The ground is made ready and then the gang comes into plant a brand new crop for the future. I'm sad to say I've never done that. I do the cutting but none of the planting. Whichever you do, it's still a fine place to work. There may not be all that much wildlife under the conifers, but there's still plenty to look at and, in the old plantations, you see foxes, pheasants and lots of other birds, and once a pair of deer, which is a rare sight up here. I hope they'll produce some fawns over the years so that we'll see more of them in the future.'

The big man turns slowly back to his work. Above him the great, black trees bend in the stiffening breeze. As evening falls rabbits begin to feed in the meadows which border the Forest. Clouds begin to build in the west and to push their way inland across the Garden of England.

ALWYNE Hawkins lives at Minnis End, Stelling Minnis. Once he was a farmer and a famous oarsman. But arthritis forced him into a wheelchair thirty years ago and since then he has been obliged to find other occupations. One of the many has been the weaving of beautiful baskets of every shape, size, colour and pattern. Not only does this give him a useful living, but it has helped to keep his hands supple and free of the crippling illness: 'This part of the world – the Minnis – has changed drastically since I was a boy. It's grown to be more or less semi-forest now, whereas it was a wide open space all the way through. I preferred it that way. All the people who lived round it could see each other. Now they tend to shut themselves in because the area is more enclosed. The other thing that's changed is that most of the people up here were small farmers, agricultural labourers and smallholders. It was a community of people whose livelihood was on the land. Nowadays very few are actively concerned with agriculture. In those old times much of Lyminge Forest was chestnut coppice. It was used by local people for making hurdles, sheep gates, fences and all that sort of thing. The chestnut was cut in rotation as it reached the right age. It was like farming it really. Every twelve years or so you came back to the same stand. And that gave work to a fair number of woodsmen up here. Slowly over the years the people, who were doing that job, died out and the coppices went with them. Not many young folk would take it on because it was a wearisome existence

When arthritis prevented Alwyne Hawkins from pursuing an active life, he discovered and perfected the art of basket weaving.

working all day and in all weathers with an axe. Not the sort of thing people want to do if they don't have to. Those times I was farming and, for the most part, living off the land. We got practically all our food off the farm, except for a few groceries. We grew our own poultry, eggs, bacon. Made our butter, cheese and got milk from the cows. We had potatoes, sprouts and all the other vegetables too. Of course, that meant that we were lucky during the War because we always had enough to eat and we could still buy our share of sugar and the other things that were rationed.'

Alwyne sits surrounded by his creations. He is thickset and bald with a round, chubby face. Close to him the kitchen stove gives off a steady heat. There is perfection in his work – the result of years of painstaking experience. He has learnt the importance of doing the job slowly, steadily and with precision. His wonderful old hand-tools are within easy reach. He is living proof of the accuracy of 'more hurry less speed': 'For the first years of arthritis I was more or less bedridden. I got fed up with doing nothing. My eyesight was going because of some treatment I had been given. So I started making corn-dollies. When I was farming we took a picture out of the old 'Farmer and Stockbreeder', which showed how to make them. Well, I'd never had time to do it before. But now I had plenty. My wife got me some corn

45

and off I went. Lots of people pulled my leg about it but I could put up with that. And I made quite a lot of them. I got better at doing it as I went along and used to send them off to the churches for Harvest Festivals. Eventually I got a bit bored with that, and started to do some cane work, which is quite similar. But I didn't find that very satisfying either. Then, quite by chance, I began to try working with willow. With the help of a primitive book and by inspecting other baskets I developed my own method of making them because I could never do them the way people told me I should. That's because my wrists are fixed and I've got limited movement in my elbows. Being in a wheelchair I just had to develop my own methods. So I've found a craft which I really enjoy. I can lose myself in it, forget I'm in the state I am and get a real sense of harmony in working with natural things. Your mind has to be tightly focused on what you're doing. Baskets don't make themselves. You need quite a lot of discipline. I'd always led an active life before and doing this is the closest I've been able to get to that sort of existence from a wheelchair. The great thing is to work with the willow – not to fight it. It has its own natural qualities. And wonderful ones they are too. I always say in my rather naive way that willow was created for making baskets; that when you work with willow you get this sense of harmony with the Creator. But you will find that many people, particularly men I must say, when they're first learning they treat it as a fight. They feel they've somehow got to overcome the willow. And you'll see that, after they've made a basket, it's not quite the shape they want. Then they'll try to force it into shape. Women are much more sympathetic to the qualities of the wood and, as a result, they do much better work with it.'

The eyes are alert and sharp as the basket grows steadily under the strong hands. The only sound is the movement of the wood. The tall strips of willow throw moving shadows against the mellow kitchen walls. Outside in the Forest it is the time of year for snowdrops and crocuses, primroses, daffodils and lambs' tails: 'It's a shame really that I can't get the willow locally. It comes all the way from Somerset. I've had it from there now for thirty-five years and more. It's a farm that grows willow and I went and stayed down there a year or two ago, had an enjoyable time. They grow it and do it up for us in bolts or bundles. A bolt of willow is the same girth at the bottom whether it's three foot, four foot, five foot or right up to ten foot long. That's how they sell it. Over the years, instead of increasing the price, they've gradually reduced the size of the bolts, which hasn't been so painful somehow. As far as the tools I work with are concerned, you don't really need that many. Basically I use a penknife, a bodkin, some secateurs, a cow's horn for greasing the bodkins and a picking knife. That's really all you want. I make my baskets to last. My wife's still got some which I made very early on. There's a clothes' basket she's had for getting on thirty years. Her shopping basket is pretty old as well. It's so tough that once, when I was in hospital, she brought me some things in it and, on her way out, she tripped over and fell on it. Well, she cracked her rib on the basket, but it didn't suffer any damage at all. The only thing about them is that you mustn't leave them on a damp floor or anywhere else like that. They really want standing up so the air can get through them. And I never varnish them. I think that's the mistake. It makes the willow brittle. The wood of the willow needs to breathe. It absorbs moisture from the atmosphere and then it dries out. Sometimes in here of a night you can hear the finished baskets creaking away – especially if you've got a fire going. They're just drying out and the sound makes you feel very much at home.'

EVERY forest needs people to look after it, to keep an eye on what is going on and to watch over its wildlife. Les Foster fulfils this role for the Forestry Commission in Lyminge Forest. He is not a man with whom you would wish to pick a fight. He is tall and broad and strong with a great black beard and challenging eyes. As he strides through the woodland with his twelve-bore over his arm and his dogs at his heels, he looks like the monarch of all he surveys: 'There are just three full-time rangers like me in the forests of Sussex and Kent. Twenty years ago there were probably twelve in the same area. There were perhaps fifty to sixty forest workers while today there are seven. So it's changed. The job is to protect the trees, to manage the wildlife and to help conservation. In the old days people like me were called warreners because of all the rabbits we had to deal with. It's more of a way of life than a job. There's certainly nothing nine to five about it. Your whole existence revolves around the work. You've got freedom even if you're not entirely your own boss. There's tasks you have to do when you're told but, in the main, you know what you've got to do and you do it the best way you can. Sometimes people have the impression that you spend all your life walking around the forest with a gun under your arm shooting everything that moves. But there's more to it than that. For one thing you need to have a lot of patience to do it well. You've got to learn to be tolerant with the public too, because there's times when they really drive you mad. Certain times of the year, particularly in the winter, when you're culling deer, you find a couple of people wandering into a plantation just as you're getting ready to shoot. But you learn to put up with it and there are lots of compensations. I was always interested in wildlife even as a kid, and I suppose you could say this job was made for me. I love being outdoors. I couldn't work in a factory. I hate towns. Out here it's quiet and peaceful. I don't mind the loneliness at all. I'll have a good natter with anybody that comes along. But working on my own doesn't bother me at all. It's a solitary job by its very nature. When you're after rabbits and in thick cover you don't want anyone else there – just your dogs, and they're good company enough. There are some operations, of course, that the more guns and dogs you have out the better it is because you can be quicker and more thorough. But that's the exception.'

The woods are full of life as Les walks slowly through the areas which have been hit by the hurricane. His dogs – a big retriever and a brown and white Jack Russell – keep close to him. The terrier jumps onto a fallen pine and tightropes along its length. The ranger's eyes and ears are alert as he covers the ground. He moves softly and quietly for such a big man: 'We're the guardians of the forest. All the time you're

47

on the look-out for anything strange or out of the ordinary. This time of the year – all the year round really – is rabbit control time. They're the main things that we've got to be on top of. The chief reason is because of the damage they do to the young trees. But they also use the forest as their home and move out from here onto the neighbouring farms. So we must take care of them for that reason too. Then, up until the end of February, we have to do the deer culling – taking out the sick and the old ones so that the rest can flourish. Once we get to April we start on squirrel control. That goes on until the end of July – sometimes as late as the end of August. It depends on how long the damage they do to the trees goes on. The moment they stop harming the oaks and beeches we stop dealing with them. They only seem to do it between April and late summer, so that's the only time we're after them. Squirrels and deer have to be shot but, with rabbits, snaring is the best and most efficient method of control. The traps are placed in a run or under a fence – wherever a rabbit goes regularly. You get your snare and, if it's properly done the rabbit dies quickly. Whatever people may say, they're quite humane.'

Les is keen on the value of the big areas of conifers, not just the hardwoods. Once they have been thinned and the light has been allowed back in, bird life returns: 'I always tell people simply to go in there, sit down and listen. Just shut your eyes and use your ears, because you'll hear far more than you'll see. It's funny about Nature and humans. People only believe what they see. But there's life among the pines. They're not as barren as they seem to be. The whole forest is teeming with wildlife. We've got badgers, foxes, voles, mice, kestrels and owls. Tawny owls in particular. I see quite a lot of those. Occasionally there are little owls as well. We've got most of the song birds too. And, of course, magpies, rooks, crows, pheasants – all the bigger birds. Each creature has got its own little corner where it lives, its own particular habitat. If things change then they go out but different ones come in to replace them. One thing we've done quite recently is to put up bat boxes. We did that in 1986 in co-operation with one of the bat groups. They said that it would probably be a year before we'd know whether there were going to be colonies of bats in them. Then the hurricane came in 1987 and, of the forty boxes that were put up, only four are left. The rest just went down with the trees. We'll get some more made now and, once everything's settled down, we'll put them back up again. Trouble is at the moment, every time we get a wind a few more trees, which were weakened in the big one, fall down. And those will probably be the ones we put the new boxes on, life being what it is. I just hope I never see damage like that storm did ever again. They tell me something like that comes round every two hundred years. I think the next one will probably be a little bit quicker than that. It was hard to believe. One day you go in and you see a stand of trees sixty, eighty, a hundred feet tall. The next day there's just stumps ten feet out of the ground or they've blown completely over and the roots are up in the air. The wildlife coped with it rather well – better than the humans I should think. In one of our forests the fallow deer rut was on. Within two days they were back roaring and groaning away as though nothing had happened.

Squirrels had a wonderful time. They were using the fallen trees like feeding tables. They hadn't got to climb to get their grub any more. It was just laying on the ground for them. They couldn't believe their luck.'

GEORGE Poile was born on the Minnis, where his mother's family has lived for generations. This is common land and an uncharacteristic part of Kent. George is in charge of the conservators and organises their flock of sheep, which graze the land round Stelling Minnis. He also runs the team which works the old windmill in the village and produces flour in the old-fashioned way: 'When I was a boy the hedges round here were cut right down to three foot and the wind used to really whip across this common. Now the trees have grown up so tall that anything from west to north-west is completely blocked and the wind just goes on over the top of the mill. So we can only grind now with the engine, except on rare occasions. That's all there is to it. It's no good my pretending it's the same thing, because I love to see the mill really going well under a good wind. That's something wonderful to look at. But you want something like thirty knots to get it going. The importance of it to me is to keep our links with the past. It's interesting for us to know how our forefathers had to work. Those times, if the wind was blowing properly, they worked all night because they knew it might have stopped the next day. They just had to keep on going while the conditions were right. Years ago they say that, from the top of this windmill, you could see seven others. Of course they've gone now. But most farms must have had one to grind their own corn. You think of the work that must have been involved. It makes things look pretty easy nowadays. Today this windmill *is* Stelling Minnis. It stands up here and crowns the village and the common. It's also my second home so I hope it will last a long time yet. It was built in 1866 so it's well over a hundred years old. The other ones probably burnt down through the stones overheating.'

The inside of the mill revives memories of below decks on a tall ship. The wood is rough and well weathered. The machinery is in good working order. George has dark hair and still retains plenty of Kent in his voice. It is a strong and sensible face and there is knowledge in it based on years of observation and experience. Perched high up on the sails and wielding a battered oil can he looks out over his beloved territory with much pride in his eyes: 'Not a bad place to be able to enjoy the Common and the Forest from. Wouldn't be so comfortable if it was blowing though. It's good country still, though it's changed a bit in my time. One thing that's different is the wildlife. When I was a boy the Common was teaming with birds and animals – rabbits, partridge, pheasant, foxes, everything. It's not the same now, though it may be starting to come back. I think it's the result of modern farming. In the old days the animals used to run off the farms onto the Common for safety. Now the farmers have sprayed and killed so many things. That's why there's less around I suppose. It's still a haven from the farmer's gun though, because nobody's allowed to shoot up here. There's just not so many creatures around to make use of it. There's more

George Poile runs the team which works the old windmill at Stelling Minnis, which was built in 1866.

human beings too, which may not help the wildlife either. Not enough old-timers left, people who appreciate this part of the world and want to preserve it. But we commoners try to keep it going as best we can. In earlier times we had to look after the area for the Lord of the Manor. But we're the bosses now. We've got all the say. Commoners have every sort of right. Like they can take firewood and bracken for their holdings. They're not meant to sell it mind. But they're allowed to use it on their own smallholdings. The other thing they can do is to graze their sheep. That's started up again quite recently. Commoners have registered and, if they've got ten acres, they're allowed to have a certain number of sheep up here. They're only turning out a few so far. About twenty people have bought a sheep each and put them into a common flock. They're all in lamb, so I'm hoping in a week or two that I'll be hearing the patter of tiny feet by the windmill. Some of the local people are pleased about the sheep. Some aren't. When they first arrived, almost everybody was against them because of having to fence their properties and to look out for them on the roads. Anyway, the flock seems to be running pretty well now and behaving properly too. So I hope there's not too much to worry about. I think it's a good thing to revive old customs and, provided we don't get too many of them, I'm sure that the sheep will do well.'

ONE of the Commoners at Stelling Minnis is Brenda Robinson, who lives at Bower Wood. She and her husband have thirty acres of woodland and fields, where they graze their sheep and goats. In addition, they keep chickens, rabbits and four dogs and three cats. Brenda produces her own cheese, yoghurt, butter, eggs, lamb, mutton and goat meat. She also spins, weaves, dyes and knits warm clothes from the fur and hair and wool of her animals: 'I like being isolated and to be surrounded by my own land and by all the animals. I particularly enjoy this place because of the woods. I always wanted to be able to put goats into a wood because they do like to browse so much. There couldn't be a better place for us really with the Common just outside the garden and Canterbury only fifteen miles away. The common rights are very useful. People who have enough land to support their animals during the winter have the right for a certain number of sheep or cattle. We're allowed to put fifty sheep out all the year round provided that we don't have a ram with them. There's lots of grass out there so it's valuable for us. And I'm pleased that more people have begun to make use of these old rules. It's reviving good things from the past, though I don't think animals like ours would probably have been seen out here in the old days. I've got three rare breeds of sheep – Soay, Shetland and Southdown. Plenty of goats too. I keep two dairy goats for household milk, quite a few pygmies and some angoras and angora crosses, which I have for spinning. On top of that there are the bantams, ducks, geese, hens and angora rabbits, whose fur I also spin. When I started out with all this I was determined that they would all pay their way. But I've got soft in my old age and mainly given up that idea. They're more like pets now, all fifty or sixty of them – or whatever there are.'

The sheep and the goats make patterns of beige, brown and white in the early spring sunshine. Brenda sits outside spinning wool for the thick, multicoloured sweaters, which will keep out any depth of cold. She has a kind face and a gentle voice. Her magnificent head of fuzzy, grey hair could well compete with her animals for use in her knitted creations. The wheel spins softly as the hard worked hands feed in the wool: 'Really I only make things for the family. I've got so many different coloured sheep that I haven't found much need for using dyes. I've just experimented with some simple things like lichen, onion skins and bracken. Only natural products of course. But the true colours are good enough for me. Then I blend in angora rabbit. I've got a goat which produces mohair and some crossbred angora goats, which give me a mixture of mohair and cashmere. So I've plenty of variety. I've also used dog hair. It's not very pleasant to spin but it's quite good when it's made up. The trouble is, as the dog is a meat-eating animal, the hair doesn't smell too fine until it's washed. But I enjoy doing it so much. You have to concentrate hard but it's very relaxing. You've got to synchronise the movement of your hands and feet. It may sound strange but it's quite a creative job. It's very peaceful out here too surrounded by the trees and all the birds and the animals. I would never go back to living in civilisation. If ever I moved it would be to somewhere even more isolated. I rather like my own company.'

PLACES like Lyminge Forest are becoming increasingly rare in the pressured South-East of England. They need to be treasured accordingly. Modern communications, industry and houses are all important. But they are not as vital as the ancient and beautiful places which they so often destroy. The poet Edward Thomas, who was killed in France in 1917, spent some of his short life in Kent and loved the country and its great beauty:

> 'It was a perfect day
> For sowing; just
> As sweet and dry was the ground
> As tobacco-dust.
>
> I tasted deep the hour
> Between the far
> Owl's chuckling first soft cry
> And the first star.
>
> A long stretched hour it was;
> Nothing undone
> Remained; the early seeds
> All safely sown.
>
> And now, hark at the rain,
> Windless and light,
> Half a kiss, half a tear
> Saying good-night.'

'It ar'n't that I loves the fox less, but that I loves the 'ound more.' *R. S. Surtees*

'Soon will the high Midsummer pomps come on,
Soon will the musk carnations break and swell,
Soon shall we have gold-dusted snapdragon,
Sweet William with his homely cottage-smell,
And stocks in fragrant blow.' *Matthew Arnold*

DITCHLING BEACON

DITCHLING Beacon stands high on the South Downs behind Brighton and commands magnificent views across the Sussex Weald to the north, and southwards away towards the English Channel. It is one of the coast's great vantage points and is the goal of many a hiker's weekend itinerary. The small, square fields and meadows of England stretch away into the mist towards Ashdown Forest, where Winnie the Pooh made his home. Nearby is a magnificent 'V' of mature trees planted to salute the Jubilee of Queen Victoria. Below the Beacon the village of Ditchling sits comfortably in a fold of the hills, its church and old houses giving it a quiet dignity, which even the invasion of London commuters has failed to destroy. This is the splendour of Sussex which Edward Thomas so much admired when he came here in the first decade of the century:

'The round unending Downs are close ahead, and upon the nearest hill a windmill beside a huge scoop in the chalk, a troop of elms below, and then low-hedged fields of grass and wheat. The farms are those of the downland. One stands at the end of the elm troop that swerves and clusters about its tiled roof, grey cliff of chimney-stack, and many gables; the stables with newer tiles; the huge slope of the barn; the low mossy cart-lodge and its wheels and grounded shafts; the pale straw stacks and the dark hay ricks with leaning ladders. A hundred sheep-bells rush by with a music of the hills in the wind. The larks are singing as if they never could have done by nightfall. It is now the hour of sunset, and windy. All the sky is soft and dark-grey-clouded except where the sun, just visible and throbbing in its own light, looks through a bright window in the west with a glow. Exactly under the sun the grass and wheat is full both of the pure effulgence and of the south-west wind, rippling and glittering: there is no sun for anything else save the water. North of the sun and out of its power lies a lush meadow, beyond it a flat marshland cut by several curves of bright water, above that a dark church on a wooded mound, and then three shadowy swoops of Down ending at a spire among trees.

South-west, the jagged ridgy cluster of a hillside town, a mill and a castle, stand dark and lucid, and behind them the mere lines of still more distant downs.'

THE Monday Group is a volunteer team of older people, who give up their afternoons on the first working day of the week, to mend, tidy and improve the paths, bridleways, fences, stiles and bridges along the Beacon. Most of them are retired and give their time and talents. Their number includes the local postman and some high-powered businessmen. The type of work done by the Group has been going on for forty-four years and, although sometimes mocked by local farmers, it is much appreciated by ramblers, riders, walkers and tourists. The men work under the watchful and benevolent eye of Harold Rowling, who was once employed as an engineer by Shell/BP: 'This particular group started work in 1982. Reg, the village postman down below, and I had been doing footpath work for many years. We felt that it was time to have a more regular commitment to the tracks, which were badly in need of attention. So we set up this weekly working party. I'm retired but Reg is still employed and he said that Monday afternoon was best for him because there's so little mail at the beginning of the week. That meant he could get away early and join the rest of us. Hence the Monday Group. On the whole we're not people who have spent our lives working in the country. Mainly we're retired people who came from office jobs. Many hadn't handled the sort of tools we use before. But they came forward willingly because they're interested in this part of the world and, as walkers, they knew the footpaths needed attention. There's also, of course, that quality in all of us which wants to leave things for the future better, if possible, than we found them. Strange to say, but the weather makes no difference to us. We work every Monday afternoon throughout the year, rain or shine. The only time we cancel is when Monday falls on Christmas Day. You'd have thought that ex-office workers would reach for their umbrellas as soon as it started to rain. But not a bit of it. They seem to enjoy working in the wet and the cold as much as on a fine spring day.'

High on the downs the men chip away at the chalk as they make good and mend. A skylark hovers and sings overhead in the deep blue of the May sky. Tweed caps, check shirts and sensible trousers are the order of the day as the team maintains its slow but steady progress. A steep hill rises above them as they work – what is almost a precipice falls away below. In all directions the green countryside of Southern England spreads to the horizon. The men have healthy, comfortable and determined faces. They have to take a good dose of exercise each week just to reach the place where they are going to work: 'I suppose that the main problem up here started during the last war. This was an army training ground and was closed off to the public. So nearly all the footpaths were barricaded with barbed wire. The result was that the whole area became badly overgrown. We started by slowly clearing the paths and opening them up after years of neglect. At the same time as we were doing that, people were becoming more affluent and thus more mobile with their cars and also more keen on walking in these lovely places. Well, there's few things more off putting than to walk a path and to find there's a rusty roll of barbed wire to climb over or a chalk-pit that you're going to slide down into if you don't take great care. Probably the farmer who owns the land won't have time to do these jobs. In any case, you can't really expect him to since it's for public recreation. It seems right for keen walkers to do the work themselves. Another thing we do a lot of is maintaining and building stiles. They're always made of oak and to a strong, standard design. You need to keep a constant eye on them because, if they become wobbly, they can be quite dangerous. We put up signs as well so that people won't get lost. Many of them are oak too. Nearly all the ones you see in this district were put up by us. More recently we've taken up bridge building and that's been great fun because it's extended our interests and given us a new challenge. We've put in about two hundred stiles now, so that's become a bit of a routine. But we love doing a bridge because it's something different and working over water is a new and interesting hazard. It's hard work certainly, but good fun too. The one we're doing at the moment is across the stream at Keymer. It's a vital link on a very popular track between the village and the downs. It's much used all the year round. So, when the old bridge fell into the stream, we were called in immediately to see what could be done. Well, we have built in oak and to our own design an eight metre span bridge. Not bad for a bunch of amateurs. Even with the water level down, it's a hard and dangerous job putting in a crossing of that length. The whole structure was built by our gang over a period of weeks down in my barn. Every component was drilled and marked up so that when we did get on site, no matter what the weather, we could put it up without making too many mistakes. When we've finished it, we shall all be very proud of it because, as it's oak, it's going to last at least twenty-five years. So it will outlive all of the group and be a memorial for us – and a very useful one too.'

Harold has lived within sight of the South Downs for over fifty years and is fascinated by the history of the area: 'Ditchling Beacon is the remnants of a neolithic fort. So, in the old documents going back to the 1430s, you'll find it called Ditchling Castle. It was the Armada that changed it. There'd been an early warning system of beacons along the coast for a century and a half before the Spaniards came. But Ditchling had not been part of it. With the new threat, it was pulled in and turned into a beacon area. People from the village were on twenty-four hour a day duty up there and, ever since, it's had the name it bears today. Personally, I wish it would go back to being called Ditchling Castle, which is more distinguished in my view. But there's not much chance of that I'm afraid. Whatever it's called, I wouldn't live anywhere else though. Nowhere else in England. Nowhere else in the world. I'd been all over the place in my job before I retired and I've seen a lot of this country too. But, in the end, this is the place for me. It's got everything – these magic downlands which are a fantastic sight as the clouds pass over the sun and throw their shadows onto the slopes. Then there's the Weald with it's different scenery – equally beautiful, and the sea over the other side. You'd have to be hard to please not to be satisfied here.'

IT is the time of year for bluebell woods and early butterflies, for fields of yellow rape reaching to the horizon, for lambs and larks and shady paths through the woods. Bert Wimborne from nearby Hurstpierpoint has seen nearly eighty such seasons and relished every one of them. He has been a gardener all his life, starting at fourteen and learning the ropes the hard way at a big house in Sussex, the county which he carries in his heart and in his voice: 'I left school in 1919 – just after the Great War and became a house-boy for six months. That was a sort of trial run to see if they thought I'd ever make a gardener. They always reckoned that, if the 'ouse-boy was any good, he'd make a useful garden boy. So, after six months, I made the grade and away I went. It was round about the end of March in those years when we got some very bad winters with frost, ice and snow. My first job was washing flower pots in cold water. I did it in an old bath tub. We had four different types of brushes for the different sorts of pots. And you had to scrub 'em really clean. I don't know about green fingers but mine were often blue with the cold. Anyway, it was a good way to learn the trade and no mistake. If you take notice when you're still a boy and show some signs that you're going to make a gardener, then they take notice of you and they'll put you with a good foreman. It might be in the lawns and pleasure areas or the rock garden, the rose garden or the vegetable garden. After you'd been with the chap for a week or so he might give you some of the rougher jobs to do on your own – spreading muck or digging or something like that. Or it could be writing out the labels. Well, if you'd took notice when you was at school, that stood you in good stead then with your spelling – even if some of the old names of the plants and shrubs were quite beyond me. Them times the labels was sawn out of wood. When we was going labelling we used to have a tin of white paint and a brush. You used to paint the piece of wood, write whatever the name was in the wet paint and then stand it up to dry. And, do you know, them old names used to stay on them labels for two or three years in spite of the foul weather we used to get.'

The old man grew up in the days when the British class system was still at its peak. He has the old-world courtesy and deference which he learnt below stairs. His eyes are still keen and wise with experience. As he hoes among the flints, song birds sun themselves in the trees above: 'I've had lots of good things from gardening, but one thing that's not so nice is a bad back. It's been like that for forty years – mainly because of the damp I should say. You see, in the good old days you was never held up by the weather or anything like that. You just kep' on dodging along. I can remember when I was about twenty-two and I was working with the foreman in the ornamental gardens round the old goldfish pond. And, by God, it was raining stair-rods. I was standing there watching the water and I said, 'Look at the rain in the pond Mr Austin'. He just went on digging away and then he replied, 'He ain't working in the pond, boy.' So I jumped back quick to my job. And I s'pose gardening outside in all those weathers is what's given me my aches and pains. We always reckoned we knew when the wet weather was coming towards the end of September because of the rooks. We called 'em Nero for a reason I don't know. Anyway, when they was flying about high in the sky like bits of burnt paper we'd say, 'Look at them old rooks winding up that water.' And, by Jove, that was about right too. Because, within a couple of hours, it would rain nearly for sure. So it was a good sign of it. Of course, we had no plastic raincoats those times. I 'ad a thick, old corn bag to keep me dry. I used to put one corner up into the other one. Have that over your head and you'd never get wet through. You could work out all day and the only place you got damp was your knees. I've worked outside all day in a storm. I've knocked off at ten

For Bert Wimborne from Hurstpierpoint, gardening has been both his profession and his hobby all his life.

to five to walk back up to the tool shed. And when I've took that old sack off it would stand upright on its own because of being almost wet through.'

As you would expect, Bert's garden is in apple-pie order. Flowers, fruit and vegetables all look ready to be shipped direct to the Chelsea Flower Show. There is steady concentration on the weathered face as the hard hands sow seeds along a string-line so taut that, if you twanged it, you would get a top A: 'After I came back from the RAF during the war I couldn't get a Head Gardener's job. Nobody had much money and them sort of occupations were thought of as a luxury. A lot of the big houses then just had a retired man, who used to try to keep the place as tidy as he could. Well, with my experience, I soon found someone who was willing to take me on for a couple of days a week. Before long I found another one like that. And then I was all set. To tell the truth, they was only too pleased to get you, specially where they had difficult things like grapes or nectarines or peaches. You see, the fruit had all grown wild, pushing up through the old glass roofs and smashing them. So, if you knew what you was doing, you could get in there in the wintertime and spend a day in some of those big greenhouses putting those vines and fruit trees back into shape. As for my own garden, it was just a bunch of rubbish when I came here. Only worthwhile thing was a row of broad beans that went across to the rose pergola. Well, I took everything down and got my little Fergie tractor and a single furrow plough and I ploughed the whole lot up except for the path. Next I got a set of discs and broke it all down and put a sub-soiler in it for drainage. After that we sat down indoors of an evening, my wife and I, and we made a plan of things. As it is today is how we planned it, within a foot or two. We put the lawn down using a mixture of grass that keeps short and healthy nearly all the time. It took five years hard toil but we got it as we wanted it in the end.'

Bert says that he would not change the life he has had, even though it has been hard and sometimes uncomfortable. Indeed, he looks back on the good old days with some regret and has little time for modern manners and inventions: 'These weed-killers and insecticides which everyone uses nowadays are a load of nonsense, if you want me to be honest. When people started using all those old chemicals that was the beginning of their gardens going backwards. You don't need all those bought things. You want muck and sprays that you mix yourself. When I was in the big gardens we used to spray for greenfly on roses. We used to use soft soap and just one drip of paraffin. We'd warm it up and then let it cool off again. Afterwards we would mix it – half a jam jar full to two gallons of water. When we sprayed it on, it'd get rid of all that old greenfly. And we'd even manage to get shot of black fly on broad beans with it. As for weeds, we never 'ad no weed-killer. We used to do it all by hand with a hoe. We wasn't allowed to have weeds. There was never any in a gentleman's garden. That's why the old gardeners got sore backs because of always bending over their hoes. The 'ead gardener he'd keep 'em at it all day. And the only chance you 'ad to straighten up was when you was working in the drive and the carriage come by. You was expected to stand up then out of respect. You wasn't asked to touch your 'at. You just had to stand up to 'em.'

DORIS Hall claims that her family has lived in the Ditchling area ever since they wore woad. She spends much of her time on a bicycle exploring and researching the ancient paths, hills and woodland. She has written books about the history of the place and the walks that can be taken there. She is a mine of information about this special part of England: 'My father was a gardener in the village and I was the third of his four children. We just had the one brother. We lived at an old house opposite the church until 1922 when my father bought an old army hut and a piece of ground. We thought we'd moved into a palace then because, at the old house, we'd had a one up and one down with a lean-to scullery. And that was for six of us with a ladder to get up into the top room. Our family history has been handed down by word of mouth almost since the days when people came down from the trees and painted themselves blue. We've always lived in the South here and lots of legends about the family have been passed along. None of my distant ancestors could read or write, no more than anyone else could in those days. And how much the stories have been distorted or added to over the years I can't tell. But there's always been a Harold Ridler in our family in every generation even up to today. And we've always been told that was because way back one of our ancestors was King Harold's fire-maker. So that's something to feel proud about. So is the village too, of course. It's a compact community and yet, within a minute, you can be out in the wide country. We've got the most beautiful walks, the most wonderful scenery and, in addition, the escarpment of the downs makes Ditchling look like a stage. We have that magnificent backdrop and all the people who have lived here over the centuries have left some type of mark on it as if they were actors in a play. I'd never go away from here. I've had many offers to leave, but I haven't taken them up. In fact, I haven't left the village for eleven years, not even for a holiday. What I would miss most would be the walks in the fields and on the hills – and the childhood memories in winter's snow or summer's sun when we used to climb up the slopes with our little tin trays and go swooshing down to the bottom. If you weren't careful you'd go straight through the hedge and tear your clothes.'

When she is writing Doris cycles out to a wooden bench close to Lodge Hill where Dickle, from whom Ditchling is said to have got its name, was supposed to have been buried. Below her is spread the splendour of Sussex, her inspiration. There are warm smile lines round the clear eyes behind the spectacles. She has a trim, fit figure, the result of sixty-five years of devotion to her bike. She has a fuzzy head of white hair. Her movements are sure and considered. She sits surrounded by the sounds of the countryside in early summer: 'I've always collected a lot of information and put it on odd scraps of paper, thinking it would come in useful one day. I never thought I'd do anything with it until, one day, my daughter said to me, 'Mummy, if you don't write this down in a book, I'll throw all these pages away.' So that's how I started. I really like to work sitting where I can see what I'm writing about. Most of my books are about this immediate area. The subjects include nature, the flowers and the birds, the village of course and some examples of Sussex folklore and logic. For instance, there's one old saying that you mustn't pick elder flowers unless you bow to the tree, because that is where the witch lives. If you don't acknowledge her, the wine goes sour. Then there's the hawthorn. So beautiful at this time of the year in May. When the berries come they're lovely and red. I always called them 'ogasses'. An old gentleman told me that it should be 'egas' and not 'ogas'. I found that odd because my ancestors always called them 'ogasses'. Anyway, he brought me a book and showed me that it was spelt with an e. So, next autumn when the berries were on the trees, I was out walking and saw an old countryman picking them. I stopped and said to him, "The egasses are ready then." "They're not egasses, they're ogasses." "Is that what you call them?' I asked. 'Yes', he said, 'eggs don't have arses, 'ogs do.' And that's one of my favourite examples of Sussex logic. Sometimes people tell me that, because I haven't had a university education, I shouldn't try to write about history. But I go to the Record Office and I cross check my facts. Another thing I do, which scholars don't bother with, is to visit old country people and to look in their family bibles. In the past, everything used to be written down and I'm allowed to read it all. If a child was born, for instance at one minute to midday it was noted down – "This child (then its name) was born at one minute to midday when the sun was high in the sky." That kind of detail gives a genuine feel for the history of ordinary people. And it's the working folk that made this country what it is. Not the university types. As far as Ditchling goes I've been able to observe it myself in my lifetime. I can say for sure that its whole character has changed in that period. When I was young there were twenty-five farms here. Now I don't think there's five. And they were mixed farms – dairy, wheat, sheep, hay, pigs, vegetables, everything. Nobody had to import any produce. And that's all gone. Then, we had three of everything in the village – three butchers' shops, three grocers, three newsagents, three greengrocers. I think they must have always gone in threes. Now we've got one butcher, a grocer and a baker. But I think the watershed came when the bank and the chemist closed. Everybody had to go out of the village for their money and their medicines. They got into the habit of shopping elsewhere. I think if those two businesses came back into Ditchling, everybody would start using the village shops again.'

After a while, Doris sets off on her bike again and travels the little lanes of her much loved county. The wild flowers and the grasses are at their finest in colour and richness. The little streams of Sussex, their water of great clarity, accompanying her with their sounds as she passes by. The downs are at their verdant best: 'Cycling keeps me fit. But I believe that health is mainly in the mind. If you keep your brain active that keeps your body active. You've got to exercise them both together. Cycling, walking, thinking, talking all combine to keep you well. The bicycle I've got at the moment is over thirty years old. We bought it for my daughter when she left

Ditchling school and had to go to Hassocks. We live eighty yards beyond the boundary where the children can take the bus. So they had to cycle. It's become my favourite means of getting about. I like the exhilaration of going downhill. You're higher up too. When you're walking, you can't see over the hedgerows. From a bicycle you can see everything on the other side. I often think that it's the secret of long life. I'm in my seventies now and I've been bicycling since I was five. It keeps your muscles tuned and your blood circulating. It keeps your brain active too because I meet a lot of people on the way. Sometimes I'm gone for two hours, but I've only done an hour's actual cycling. I'm a talkative person and, although I doubt that I've got the sort of face that makes people want to talk to me, they seem to want to anyway. Another thing I like to do when I'm out is to clip flower seeds. I take a little bag to keep them in and, if I see a place that has no wild flowers, I scatter the seeds round the banks or in the woods. Then I go back about two years later and see a lovely spread of bluebells or honesty, which is one of my favourites. It's a truly wild flower from the start. In this way, I believe we're really helping nature. Just as long as people don't throw wild seeds into ploughed fields where crops are going to grow, because they get into the combine harvester and they have a sap in them which rather clogs up the works. Now we're beginning to get flowers back which had nearly died out and which my grand-children would not have seen. I'm so happy to be able to do my little bit for future generations.'

A FINE bakery has stood in West Street, Ditchling for more than a hundred years. The bread shop which went with the bakery used to be one of the centres of village life. Later it became run-down and less popular. Today it is called Dolly's Pantry and is run with style and distinction by Siobhan Barrett: 'We inherited the name of the shop from our predecessors. We thought it was rather quaint so we decided to keep it. I believe every village needs its individual stores rather than supermarkets. A village bakery is traditional and we try to encourage local people to use it. The tea room we've added as an extra and we hope that villagers will bring their friends. Also that tourists and people passing through will come in and enjoy what we have to offer. We even do a weekly senior citizens lunch, which is quite popular. So I think you could argue that we offer something worthwhile to the life of the village. It's not always easy and it takes time, but I'd say we're on the way up. Going back a few years now I remember thinking that there was a lot more you could do for the community here, to bring it together and to improve its spirit. And I think that's happening now. Our trade is unpredictable. In spite of that we've tried to work out a pattern for the way we operate. You need that if you can manage it. There aren't many flat periods. We're busy most of the year round and especially on Bank Holidays. We're open seven days a week from eight o'clock in the morning until six in the evening. In the summer we plan to stay open later. We also do private functions and outside catering, so there's a lot we can do from here, using the shop as a base. It's surprising too from how far afield people come. We get customers from Southampton who come back every time they're visiting the area. Others from Oxford who make a point of dropping in. But mainly they come from Ditchling and the surrounding area. Visitors have quite often said to me that their village doesn't have this sort of place and that they miss it. So I think they're pleased to find us because it reminds them of times past.'

The shop is neat and clean and tidy. Trim tables are laid with gleaming china and cutlery. The unique smell of fresh-baked bread creeps into every nook and cranny. In the bakery skilled hands knead dough and turn out crusty loaves of every shape and size. Experienced fingers plump fresh strawberries into the top of cream cakes. And thick coats of scarlet jam are spread wantonly on sheets of yellow pastry. Siobhan, with her tawny hair and handsome face, keeps a quiet eye on both sides of the counter: 'Noel is my baker and he's really excellent. We rely on him. He produces the bread and the cakes and can turn his hand to anything that's needed. Like most bakers he works awfully long hours. He normally starts at five o'clock in the morning. At weekends he starts at midnight and works through until eleven on a Saturday. Other days he stays on until four o'clock in the afternoon. It really just depends what's needed. One of my weaknesses is that I like to try the bread myself. It's an interesting art making it and there are so many things that you can do with dough. You can mould it into curious shapes and make quite unusual things out of it. So we try to be as creative as we can and to make everything we produce look attractive as well as tasting really good. In that way I hope the shop is welcoming. There's a trend now, I believe, towards traditional things – home baking and cooking. That's what we're trying to achieve. And what better place to do it than a country village? It's so relaxed here and the scenery so beautiful. I prefer this to the seaside. There are so many different things going on. And all the birds and flowers and wildlife too.'

NOT much that is made at Dolly's Pantry goes unsold. What there is is collected each day by Michael Alford from East End Lane Farm. There it is fed to the lucky ducks, geese and swans on his lake, where he has started a bird sanctuary. Michael's family has farmed in Ditchling for over fifty years. Now he is hoping to turn the whole enterprise into a Nature Park. As a foundation, he has an extensive collection of photographs of the Ditchling area going back for over a century. He plans to use them for an exhibition in one of his barns along with a collection of old farm implements: 'The family's been here since 1929. My grandfather came up with his two sons and started farming. At that time it was mainly a milking herd with Guernsey cows. My grandfather died about two years after my father took the farm over with his brother, Tom. They farmed right on through. Then, when I was old enough, I worked with my Dad until his death. We had milking cows up until 1975 when I changed over to beef animals. Now, with this nature reserve idea, we're changing again. I wanted to do something that would satisfy me and also earn a decent living. I like the idea of rare cattle and pigs and a pond with beautiful birds on

64

Michael Alford's family have farmed in Ditchling for over fifty years. Michael takes care of many birds at his bird sanctuary.

it. I think I'll find it all very satisfying. One alternative was to let them build houses here. But I couldn't really bear that. I'd like it to be something that can be carried on into future generations. I hope my family may want to keep it going. Eventually there's going to be seven or eight ponds – big and small – with all the wildlife and birds you can imagine. Animals everywhere too, and all the things that are to do with this lovely countryside.'

Michael's hair is grey and his arms and face strong and sun-tanned. He is a sturdy and resilient man, who makes up his own mind about things and who sticks to what he knows. It is a sadness that men like him seem no longer needed to produce food for the citizens of Sussex. But it is entirely predictable that they find other and imaginative ways of making use of their precious land: 'We've got two whooping swans which were given to me by a friend. They're special to me and they breed very well here. They've already reared some cygnets and brought them up. We've managed to sell or swap the young ones and so to bring other geese and ducks onto the ponds, which helps finance the operation. The female is sitting on some more eggs now. Every day I go down to feed her and her mate with a bit of bread or corn. I go across to the nest just to check that she's OK and doing well. When I get close she stands up and looks at me and makes a bit of a noise. The cob comes flying straight across to see what's going on. They make the hell of a racket living up to their whooping name for a while, but they soon settle back to their normal way of life. They know me because they see me walking past all the time. So they get used to me. If anybody strange went across to them the male would really go for them and hit them hard, I'm sure. They couldn't break your arms or legs unless you were weak-boned. But they could hurt you just the same. Same with the geese too. I've had a quite small barnacle goose get angry enough to fly and jump on my back when I've been trying to look at the nest. They get quite vicious at that time of the year. The pleasing thing about it all is that we're bringing in now a lot of water birds, which were never round this area at all. As we breed on I hope that even more will be tempted to join us so that as time goes on more and more different birds will be brought to these ponds and lakes.'

IN 1832 William Cobbett, that great rural rider, visited Newcastle-upon-Tyne and, from there, launched a savage attack on agricultural conditions on the Sussex Downs, which he had last visited in the Summer of 1823. By comparison with his diatribe today's farming conditions seem quite mild:

'If any of these sensible men of Newcastle were to see the farming in the South Downs, and to see, as I saw in the month of July last, four teams of large oxen, six in a team, all ploughing in one field in preparation for wheat, and several pairs of horses, in the same field, dragging, harrowing, and rolling, and has seen on the other side of the road from five to six quarters of wheat standing upon the acre, and from nine to ten quarters of oats standing along side of it, each of the two fields from fifty to a hundred statute acres; if any of these sensible men of Newcastle could see these things, they would laugh at the childish work that they see going on here under the name of farming; the very sight would make them feel how imperious is the duty on the law-giver to prevent distress from visiting the fields, and to take care that those whose labour produced all the food and all the raiment, shall not be fed upon potatoes and covered with rags; contemplating the important effects of their labour, each man of them could say as I said when this mean and savage faction had me at my trial, 'I would see all these labourers hanged, and be hanged along with them, rather than see them live upon potatoes.'

WALLAND MARSH

WALLAND Marsh straddles the Kent and Sussex borders and makes up a third of the area better known as Romney Marsh – a great arrow-head of land piercing its way out into the western wing of the Straits of Dover. This is traditional smugglers' country and much of the atmosphere of those turbulent times remains. On the low country at night when the mist is rolling in from the sea, it is not hard to imagine the triumphs and terrors, the victories and the violence of those far-off days. There are still men who dare to whisper that such things continue now – though with booty more lethal than brandy, tobacco and silk.

The fine village of Appledore is the gateway to the Marsh, and it was here that William Cobbett came in the late summer of 1823: 'From Tenterden I set off at five o'clock and got to Appledore after a most delightful ride – the high land upon my right and the low land of the Walland Marsh on my left. The fog was so thick and white along some of the low land that I should have taken it for water, if little hills and trees had not risen up through it here and there. In quitting Appledore I crossed a canal and entered the Marsh. This was grassland on both sides of me to a great distance. The flocks and herds immense. The faces of the sheep are white and, indeed, the whole sheep is as white as a piece of writing-paper.'

JIM Pilcher and his brother Joe farm 200 acres of the Walland Marsh at Creek End, East Guldeford and on the edge of the County borders. They are true marshmen and have links with shepherds and lookers going back through the centuries. Sometimes they still shear their sheep with the old-fashioned equipment, which they collect and cherish: 'This hand-shearing makes me puff. Mind you, anything makes me puff at my age. I first started to shear about fifty years ago, and I've been doing it ever since. Nowadays I don't do our whole flock though. The contractors come in to do that. I just tinker about but I get a hell of a kick out of using these old machines and showing people how the job used to be done. Them days we'd only shear our own and a few for the neighbours. That would be a thousand or fifteen hundred. We'd spend three weeks at it before harvest. But that was nothing to what the professionals do now. I mean the Australians and the Kiwis come over here and even our local lads go all over the world shearing. They do more sheep in a year than I've done in a lifetime. Of course, to be fair to me, the gear's entirely different now. It's an electric machine that hangs up in the air and the shafting comes straight down and the chap just does the job. He doesn't even have to wind up the wool afterwards. There's somebody else to do that. But I would say that it's not as interesting as working with these old machines, although they'd take the fleece off similar to me. I'd claim that my sheep look slightly better afterwards – though the animals don't seem to mind too much about that. But the butchers used to. Years ago, so father said, they'd always give sixpence more for a well-shorn sheep. They'd look around, if it were a bit rough, and ask, 'Who sheared that?' They believed that if it was well shorn it was the sign of a careful shepherd that had taken trouble to look after his sheep. And you remember, that extra sixpence was a lot of money in the 1930s. The butchers didn't like to see the skin nicked by the shearer for instance. It was the butcher's job to take the skin off and to carve the animal and the shepherd's to take the wool off and the wool alone.'

While Joe winds a handle as big as a bicycle wheel to make the blades run, Jim firmly but gently manoeuvres each animal into position so that he can give it the treatment: 'You never ill-treat a sheep when you're shearing it because it's going to struggle all the more. You might cuss it a bit under your breath but you've got to hang on and make a good job of it. It's a most difficult thing to learn because it's a live animal, each one is slightly different and you've got a very dangerous and sharp tool you're working with – although if you use it properly you can't cut the sheep. So you're tensed up to react to that very slight movement when you know she's going to struggle and you're going to have to tighten your grip. It's hot, it's heavy and it's greasy and you're strained mentally as well as physically. You see, you've only got your knees and one arm to control her – the other arm is doing the cutting. And I have to admit that the bit I enjoy most is when the last one's turned out shorn. Always did. I hated the job as a young chap and then grew to like it more because it was a way to earn a bit of extra money. Then as I got older I went into farming with my brother, who still sees to our sheep more than me. Though I always came in for the shearing part of the job. Next I started collecting old shearing equipment and then twenty years ago someone asked me to demonstrate at a Traction Engine Rally and it fascinated me that did. People would stand and watch me and, being a bit of a show off, it gave me a hell of a thrill to be able to show an old country skill so that lots of people wanted to come along to see how it was done.'

The rich folds of wool – dirty grey on the outside, pure white on the inside – spread themselves on the ground beside the big Kent ewe. Gone in a few minutes is the coat which has protected her from the rigours of a winter on the Marsh. She looks half the size when she springs free at the end relieved of her burden and happy to be cool in the summer heat: 'We want the meat of course and that's the main return in sheep farming. But the wool is a very important by-product too. An interesting fact is that all the time there is paper being made, we're in the market with our wool. It's not just sweaters and cardigans you see. Without us there's nothing to make felt and they have to have felt to make paper. When it's in process it goes through rollers to have the water squeezed out and the rollers are clad in woollen felt. This squeezes out the water again and again and does it millions of times without losing its water holding quality or its springiness. That's one big use of wool which people don't know about, but there's scores of them. Sometimes I'm working close to the flight-path of Concorde. And when she goes over nobody pays

Jim Pilcher farms at Greek End on the broad flatlands of Walland Marsh with his brother Joe.

much attention because it's an everyday event for them. But I stop in the middle of shearing and say to the people who are watching that Concorde and I have got something in common. Because the seats in the aeroplane are covered with hundred percent woollen fibre. There's nothing for comfort, pleasure and fire-resistance compared to wool. And there's even a three million to one chance that I might have shorn the wool that's on those seats.'

The land which the Pilcher brothers farm is as flat as a bread board. Every now and then a small shepherd's hut breaks the horizon. Deep dykes divide the fields and meadows. Few trees grow here, but wonderful crops do: 'It's world famous this land. Pre-war there was only New Zealand that kept the same amount of sheep per acre. The Romans started the farming here and kept the sea back and the taming process slowly crept this way. We were the last of the Marsh to be reclaimed here. And gradually it all dried out. Of course, when you've got fields with a history of four hundred years of sheep on them and nothing else, centuries of dung and growth and grazing, it makes such marvellous pastures. All right, it gets a bit chilly out here in the winter and we suffer a lot from the wind. But these Romney sheep have got quite used to it over the generations, and there's nothing to beat them for putting up with the weather and the wet conditions we have in the bad months. Down this end of the Marsh – the Walland – there are still more sheep than there are anywhere else. The eastern end has all been ploughed up – and a lot this way too. On our acres we're half arable and half sheep. So we've got the ewes, and then we grow something like sixty acres of wheat, twenty-five acres of peas and then we've got a specialist crop of Kentish wild white clover mixed with Kent indigenous rye grass. It's used for seed to plant on the sheep-grazing meadows to give them their grub. We help the pollination along with the clover by letting a bloke from Petham near Canterbury bring his bees down here. He has twenty or thirty hives and it helps our crop and gives him some rather nice honey too.'

Jim strides off across his land. He is fit and hard, his face wind-tanned and leathery with deep smile lines round the eyes, which scan the sheep as he passes by. This is not country for anyone who wants things easy. But there is a satisfaction, unknown to most city folk, in achieving good results against the odds and in spite of the elements.

BERYL Catt lives in the old lock-keeper's cottage at Iden Lock, not far cross-country from where the Pilchers have their farm. It would be a difficult journey nonetheless because of all the wide dykes which you would need to cross. Miss Catt, who is now in her eighties, comes from one of the oldest of the Marsh families and wouldn't dream of living anywhere else: 'The Marsh is our life, I suppose. It's hard to explain why. It's just inside us, an instinct for its open spaces. We're a bit crazy about it really and one thing we don't like is trees too close to us. We like them at a distance, but not to shut you in. I can tell you a story about a man who lived on an isolated spot on the Marsh. He had a job offered him up on the hill above the flat

Langstone Harbour lies close to the multitudes of Fareham, Portsmouth and Havant. But it is still, thank heaven, a haven for wildlife and birds of every make and description. This flock of smart, black and white dinner-jacketed oyster catchers is one of the regular encouraging sights over these much exploited waters.

'The stag at eve had drunk his fill,
Where danced the moon on Monan's rill,
And deep his midnight lair had made
In lone Glenartney's hazel shade.'   *Sir Walter Scott*

Beryl Catt, who comes from one of the oldest Marsh families, is lucky enough to live in the lock keeper's cottage at Iden Lock on the Kent-Sussex border.

lands and, after thinking about it, he took it. Well, after he'd been there a while a mate of his saw him and asked him how he was liking his new work. And he said to him, 'I've got a good job. I've got a nice boss. I like my workmates and we have a comfy house – nice for my missus because we're right on the bus route and that helps a lot because it's easy for the children to get to school. But I don't think I can stand it another month because, when I go outside, all I can see is trees.' And he came back on the Marsh into much worse conditions and was happy again. Explain it how you will, but that's typical of us people down here.'

In spite of her years Beryl Catt still goes out walking along the edge of the great canal beside her house, which was dug along the top of the marsh to repel an expected invasion by Napoleon. Yellow lilies clad the surface of the water. Swallows skim and feed. Butterflies float through the still air. Above, the sky is unbroken blue. The frail but stalwart old lady tramps the margin and enjoys the sights, the sounds and the smells: 'I'm lucky and I know it to live in such a place. My house is just in Sussex. Kent is half-a-mile up the road. You can see the difference very plainly. The road in Kent is better 'cos it's much wealthier than Sussex. There's a boundary stone up on the bank at the border, but the fishermen who come here all insist that I live in Kent, which makes me a bit cross because I'm proud to live in Sussex. I tell them they're wrong but it doesn't convince them. This must be Kent to them because they come in through Appledore, which is in Kent and so this has got to be too. I think it's right to have a proper pride in your county. I don't know for sure that mine is better than next door, but I'm sure they would think theirs was the best. But if you live your whole life in a place I think you're going to believe it's special. When I was a child – over eighty years ago now – this was a different place and even more attractive, because none of the Marsh was ploughed then. It was all grazing, all sheep. We never saw anything else. It wasn't until the War when it was essential to grow corn that it all changed. Then everything got cultivated. Now some of it has gone back again but much of it is still crops. We old 'uns liked it better in those days, but that's old age for you, isn't it? Of course, it was a bit bleak and isolated in those times. But you were brought up to be used to it and you didn't take any notice. In fact, my father used to say that the only shelter we had in these parts was Lydd Church, which is quite a long way away. And it wasn't much shelter in any case. Everything was so different then. There was no mains water. No cars, of course. I remember getting very excited when I saw a car along the road. There was just the odd horse and cart and a man sitting up in it with his whip. As often as not he'd be drunk. And that was all the traffic we had. We walked to school and back every day and you couldn't let children do that today what with the traffic and the strange people there are around. I suppose I shouldn't much like to go back to it now without electricity and running water and those things. But part of me would. The world seemed a safer place then.'

The old eyes smile as they remember. The sun reflects off the calm water. In the distance a heron flaps honking into the sky and the sounds of distant tractors grumble across the Walland.

JIM Baker is a retired Marsh water bailiff. He still keeps a bunch of Romney sheep in his meadow to remind him of his days on the Walland. He is in his late seventies now and is enjoying having a bit of a rest. But he still likes to visit the places where he used to work and to watch his successors keeping the waterways clear and flowing. He too has strong and colourful memories of the old times: 'I was born down there on the Marsh in the days when sheep ruled. And I'm not so pleased to see what's happened since with all the ploughing and the crops. Course, the drainage has changed entirely since them days. All the land drain works was done by 'and labour. We had nothing mechanical – nothing at all. Most of the work then was done by contract labour and I was foreman in charge of gangs of men working in the ditches. We used strange old tools – one called a mudding trug which was handy for shovelling the wet mud up onto the banks of the sewers. And our spades were made of wood – blade and all. Not made in factories but by the local wheelwright – and I've still got 'em. And they're still usable. I've got one which goes back to 1921 but others a lot further than that. In those days there was a lot of weed-cutting to do, and back-breaking work it was as well. But the main thing to do was always to keep the waterways clear so that the Marsh would stay drained. That's always been the priority. It meant in the autumn time cutting all the summer growth from the rivers so that there was nothing to hold back the flood waters in the winter months. Those days we had some bad years when it flooded even though we'd done all the necessary work. That was before the pumping stations was built. They're one modern thing that the Walland has benefited from a lot.'

The old man has a sing-song in his voice and the vowels are South-East soft. His face is lean and his eyes alert as he trims the hedge in front of his cottage. It is early yet and the heat is still at bay. In the meadow his small flock of sheep grazes quietly under a perfectly formed oak tree, which has stood there for a couple of hundred years: 'Once you've been on the Marsh in your young days, you don't want to leave it. I remember some folk going away but almost all of them have drifted back now. I can't explain it really. It's some instinct I think. Some that are bred here don't care for trees or for the uplands. But there's more to it than that. It just pulls you back in spite of the wet and the wind and the dangers. I'll never forget 1960, which was the last really bad flood we've 'ad on the Walland. The roads were all under water and it was like a lake practically, cliff to cliff right the way across. Luckily, they managed to get all the livestock off in time. It reminded me of what happened in the War when we was all evacuated. It was compulsory because of the risk of an invasion. All the people and all the sheep was taken away from the coast – and the cattle too. Great flocks and herds were on the move. They went anywheres up onto the high ground – chiefly into Sussex and Surrey. It wasn't too difficult because people had got used to doing that when there was flood danger in the winter, so the neighbouring counties were quite accustomed to a lot of Marsh animals arriving to graze. Another memory I have is of slipping off the sluice on a very cold day and going right down into the water. As I got out a lady who was standing there said to me: 'The best thing you can do is to go home, run back as quickly as you can and change. Don't get cold!' Well, it was a bit late for that because I was cold enough already. She had no blanket or anything so off I went. But, even though I ran the whole way, I didn't feel much warmer.'

WOODCHURCH is a few miles to the north of the Walland Marsh and the next village up from Appledore. Here, at Church Elms, Fran Geering looks after a mixed bag of rare breeds. Mid-July is Kent Show time, so Fran and her family and friends are hard at work scrubbing, polishing, grooming and training her precious charges for the show-ring, where she has already won a good number of prizes. 'This whole thing started two days after we got back from our honeymoon when we bought our first Jersey calf. We reared her and called her Sophie because we'd been to Italy and thought her big, black eyes made her look like Sophia Loren. And it all escalated from there. We began by rearing more calves. Then I got interested in the rare breeds, because I felt that on a small farm it would be more fun and more interesting to do something specialised, so I found some Dexter cattle. They're an ideal smallholder's cow. They're small, they don't eat too much and they don't need many acres of land. Then we got some Jacob sheep, which aren't particularly rare. But that led me on to sheep from the Isle of Man – the indigenous breed there – and very unusual too. I fell in love with them. Next it was Shetland sheep – and I can't even remember why now. My husband decided that he would like to have pigs, and in 1985 we went up to the Rare Breeds Survival Trust and chose Elizabeth. She was an in-pig Tamworth gilt and my husband was very pleased because he's wanted to have Tamworths with their lovely, golden colour. He's very long-suffering with all my Noah's Ark, so I'm glad to let him have his say when I can. And I'm glad he chose these pigs because, now we've learnt about them, they've become my favourites too. We've been here twenty years and the whole thing's just grown like Topsy.'

The farmyard is alive with children, animals, doves, splashing water, the clanking of feed buckets and the scurrying of feet. A big bruiser of a cat watches the scene with superior scorn. In the meadow a tiny blonde girl is struggling to persuade a horned sheep to practice walking in circles for the show-ring: 'To be honest, there's not much time to do anything other than to look after the farm and to care for my four children. That's my life and I don't regret it at all. It's in my blood and it's what makes me tick. I can't imagine living in any other way. Although family life does suffer to some extent when I'm up to my eyes in lambing or showing or whatever else it may be and they have to take second fiddle, there are compensations. For example, there is the pleasure of walking over your own fields in the evening. There's a lake across one of the meadows and there are often geese on it. Yesterday we watched a fox crossing a field in the dusk. Sights like that have to be treasured. Then sometimes I win a prize in the ring and the family basks in my reflected glory. The children too benefit a lot by seeing life and nature in the raw. They see life, birth, death, sickness – the whole cycle – which I think is very good for them. And they develop a sense of responsibility in caring for the stock, which is healthy too. They're right in the midst of the activity here at the moment while we're getting ready for the County Show at Maidstone. We're in it in strength this year. We've entered cattle, sheep and pigs. So we're all heavily involved. Most people seem to enter one or the other, but seldom all three because it involves a great deal of running up and down the show ground from one set of animal lines to the other. My daughter, Emma looks after the cattle for me. She's going to be showing the three Dexters – two cows with calves at foot and one in-calf heifer. And, in the Young Farmers Class, she's showing her Belgian Blue cross Friesian bullock. She won that class last year so she's working very hard this time to try to achieve the same result. She's been away at college this year, so she hasn't really had the time to devote to him that she would like to have done. So it's a bit of a last minute panic. In spite of that he's looking very well indeed. Meantime, I've been getting the calves walking out on halters and we've now got to the stage where Ruth, who's still quite small, can lead it around. It's not too strong for her now and she absolutely adores doing it. Whether we can find a white coat tiny enough for her to wear and to show the calf in the ring we'll have to wait and see. But I know that's what she would like to be able to do. Adam's very good at helping with the pigs. He helps with the feeding and enjoys walking them round. So we'll just have to see what happens on Thursday, which is the big judging day. We'll have a very early start in the morning getting up soon after four to feed the rest of the stock on the farm before we leave for the show ground where judging starts at nine o'clock sharp. When we get there we have to feed everything. After that, the washing, brushing and grooming all start. And then, at the last minute, the white coats come out and into the ring we go. I'm planning to show the sheep but I've had some back trouble so we'll just have to see how that gets on. Emma will do her cattle, of course. I don't think Adam's quite ready yet to show the Tamworth gilt, though he should be in a year or two. So I may have to do that one as well. But I want them all to be involved because it helps their interest and it gives them that feeling that they've really achieved something worthwhile. And it doesn't really matter whether we come out with a coloured ribbon or not. After that, we pack everything up — winners or losers — and head back to the farm. It's always good coming home. We all of us love living above the Romney and the Walland Marshes. We're on the edge and I'd like to live even closer. But this will do. The land is clay and wet and sticky in the winter, rock hard in summer. So it's not an easy living. But there's an ancient sense of timelessness about the place which is very precious. I like flat country too. I'm not a hill person, though I enjoy visiting the ruggedness of Scotland. I love the openness of the Marsh, the big skies, the cloud formations, the dawns and the sunsets.'

FRANCES Smith's home is on Appledore Heath close to the north of Walland Marsh. Frances is a keen gardener and, because of that, she has found a way of making a living while catering for gourmet palates in London and across the South-East. With the help of her husband Neil and local man Robin Gill, she grows scores of varieties of specialist vegetables for some of the most demanding chefs in the business: 'Our business began a few years ago when restaurant owners and their chefs were complaining that they couldn't get the small vegetables that they really wanted. They couldn't find all the herbs either. The two things most in demand were baby leeks and flat parsley. And the whole thing really began with just those two. Well, chefs talk to one another of course and as it became known that we were prepared to grow to order we began to get the phone calls and to do the growing. Over a period of two years, it extended from our back garden to the rows of tunnels we've got now. We started the tunnels because one winter a chef complained that we had let him down because the frost had got his parsley. He wanted to know why it hadn't been covered up. So we built a tunnel, which paid for the next one. And so it went on. Of course, the main thing about all this is that I absolutely love gardening. I've always been a gardener. Started when I was sixteen on a roof garden in London. Had an allotment when we had a house in Beckenham. And we've always grown our own vegetables here. It was those ones that our first chef saw and wanted. The other thing is that Kent is the perfect place to grow stuff. It's the Garden of England. All the soils in Kent as far as I know will grow something. When we first moved here the Ministry of Agriculture was called in. We asked them what we ought to do with the land. The girl who came was quite excited and told me that I could grow anything I wanted here. And I think I've proved her right – and will continue to do so.'

The long, white tunnels are full to overflowing with plants and vegetables, some of which you recognise and some of which you don't. One area is like a tropical rain forest with water cascading down from the roof and beading the leaves with its fine droplets. The sun is already producing heat and there is a smell of richness and abundance. Frances and her team move steadily through the beds picking three bags of one thing, perhaps five of another. They work quietly and calmly. Distant sheep call from the direction of Walland Marsh: 'This morning we're doing the Wednesday pick. That involves gathering together all the herbs and the leaves that we need for the seven customers whom we service today. Some are in the tunnels, some are outside. The Wednesday run goes all the way to Brighton. It starts in Rye and then we go to Hastings, Battle, Eastbourne and Lewes before ending up in Brighton. Then we come back via Robertsbridge. All the customers today are restaurants. Some days we have fishmongers and delicatessens as well. The restaurants range from the Bistro in Rye, which is a small, intimate place, to some very high class ones at the top of the range in Brighton. We carry stocks of about two hundred different varieties of seeds and I believe I have grown as many as three hundred different things since we started. Some come, some go. We always aim to have about thirty different leaves available and that carries on even in the winter. We grow all the standard herbs of course and some that are not quite so usual. There's great satisfaction in growing so many different things because no two people – and even more particularly no two chefs – are alike. What is stupid is if everyone has to cook with the same dreary product or if each restaurant has to serve up the same sad, little salad. When people come here they can create their own salad to precisely their own requirements from a wide selection of leaves. Maybe they'll only want one or two of the unusual ones, but it will make their food different. One of the good things for us is that our customers seem to love coming to visit us here. Although everyone is dreadfully busy nowadays they get round to it sooner or later. Once a year we try to have them all over for lunch and let them go on nibbling safaris through the tunnels, which are very popular. It gives them a chance to see and to taste things which they may have turned down at first acquaintance. They can have another look. Or they may find new things that I wasn't growing the last time they came. In any case, it all helps to encourage business.'

The work continues relentlessly. Neil Smith wears a Panama hat against the steady glare of the July sunshine as he selects wild strawberries for classy customers. Frances bustles to and fro, picking, exhorting, encouraging, while Robin Gill piles the boxes of produce in a tempting leaning tower of Pisa: 'All the tunnels are divided into little squares because the ideal way of growing stuff as organically as we try to is that you control your pests and diseases naturally. Each square being quite different from its neighbour stops pests rampaging from one end of the tunnel to the other. Also it means that I can designate patches as belonging to one customer or to another, which means that you are less likely to run out of things which may be in short supply. We tend to be phoned up by people who want far too much of things that are scarce. For instance, we never seem to be able to grow enough tarragon. There's always too little basil or too few baby carrots. They're all very popular and, sadly, not all that profitable. We do them very much as a favour to favoured customers. The other problem we sometimes have is when you get people who urgently demand the most enormous quantities of things which we're just not geared up to supply. We can't do bulk orders. We specialise in looking after the small people, who don't want masses and masses of unusual produce. In the main, people are very understanding and helpful though and we feel lucky with our customers.'

In the high summer the birds at the Rye Harbour Nature Reserve just down the coast are basking in the sunshine and trying to recover from a breeding season decimated by marauding foxes. At sea, a scarlet fishing boat rides the swell as it makes for the harbour mouth. On the marshland tractors are starting to cultivate after an early harvest. And in the sky gulls wheel and cry as they search for food.

HISTORY has laid its hand again and again on these old marshes. The Romans landed along the shoreline and marched north from here. In a storm far greater than the hurricane of 1987 and before global warming and its imagined effect on the weather was even dreamed of, the green pastures vanished under the sea in 1286. The Royal Military Canal was dug to repel an anticipated invasion by Napoleon and, in the Second World War, this was considered the most likely place for a German, sea-borne invasion. In spite of turmoil and threats, the true marsh people have managed to hang on to their pride and their privacy. Their loyalty to their patch is unquenchable. They may not always know why they love this low, flat, damp, windy place. But they know that it is theirs and that they will stay.

CHICHESTER AND LANGSTONE HARBOURS

CHICHESTER and Langstone Harbours lie side by side in the centre of the south coast and close to the north-east of the Isle of Wight. Both have many claims to fame. Both are much loved by yachtsmen and fishermen. Both possess some of the best opportunities for bird-watching anywhere in the country. Langstone is more hard pressed with the busy city of Portsmouth making up its western boundary. Hundreds of thousands of people, industry, the navy and the bustling activity along the coast mean that pollution, sewage and building have all threatened the harbour's future. The area is made up of a series of low-lying islands and peninsulas between which lie marshy harbours crossed by creeks and channels. Its outline has altered over the centuries because of silting. Chichester Harbour is quieter, more mysterious. Its narrow entrance between Hayling Island and East Head opens out into a land-locked lagoon, where peninsulas split the main channel into several tidal creeks. It is a place for exploring and for Arthur Ransome adventures.

FROM high on the downs behind Chichester a grand, old Alvis motor-car makes its way sedately towards the sea. It was built in the days when elegance still mattered and before people were willing to be seen in public in characterless, metal coffins. Behind the wheel sits the heavily-bearded figure of Richard Williamson, Reserve Warden for the Nature Conservancy Council at Kingley Vale. On top of the downs Richard is in charge of one of the world's great yew forests and a galaxy of wildlife, birds and butterflies. His patch commands some of the great views in Britain. On fine days he can take in at a glance the whole spread of the south coast, which includes Chichester Harbour, Langstone Harbour and out to the Isle of Wight. On his infrequent days off he likes to climb into the Alvis and head for the sea to enjoy the bird life and the natural history of the coastline: 'I've known and loved Chichester Harbour for more than twenty-five years. There's so much to look at, especially on a fine summer's day. The lovely boats full of happy people, the birds, the flowers, the water and the scenery. It's just the place for a day out – but you need to know your way around. One of my favourite places is at Fishbourne. It's a mile to the west of Chichester and the Romans built a magnificent palace there, which you can still visit today. There's also a nature reserve, which is run by the Chichester Harbour Wildfowlers. From the Reserve you can see the masts of the sailing boats way down the Channel as far as Dell Quay. You can also see and watch plenty of black-headed gulls. They're one of the commonest birds in the harbour. They breed in the Baltic and in Holland and they come down here in the early autumn. They've got their young ones with them and they'll be spending the whole of the winter here. Sometimes we get as many as twenty or thirty thousand of them. You can tell the young ones because of their brown plumage streaks. The adults have just started to lose their black face masks, from which the birds get their name and which they have during the breeding season. They do a lot of preening and bathing, dipping their heads down into the water and splashing about. Amongst them are some common gulls too. Not perhaps the most exciting of scenes but it satisfies me because I get as much pleasure from the ordinary as I do from the extraordinary.'

Fishbourne boasts tall stands of strong and supple reeds, which guard the water-line and give cover to many kinds of birds. They also offer helpful hiding places to those humans wishing to observe them: 'I have a special feeling for these reed beds. Perhaps it's why I like this place so much. Although it's called the common reed, it's other name is Norfolk reed. And the whole of the Norfolk Broads, where I come from, are covered by them. It's a lovely soothing experience to be in a reed bed. It's never silent. It's never still. It's always moving. And there's something about it which is very lulling and powerful at the same time. You wouldn't believe it, but this is the tallest grass in the world – even if it doesn't look like it. In Britain I suppose it grows to about eight feet or so in height. But in the Euphrates marshes in Iraq, which are massive in area, it grows so tall that it's used as a mast in their boats. The shorter ones they use for punt poles. They don't just make them into thatch for their roofs like we do either. They use them in the structure of their buildings in the floating villages they inhabit on the marshes. As far as I am concerned here at Fishbourne, they simply make an excellent look-out point for me to watch what's going on. Sometimes you can see some quite exciting birds like the water-rail. That's the first cousin of the corncrake. Often there are moorhens, which are like water-rails, but a little bit bigger. Then there are reed warblers, reed buntings and sedge warblers. It's a good place for herons too. There are several breeding lower down in one of the woods. This time of year the young are out looking around for food in the channels. We have twenty or thirty pairs here I suppose. The folk name for heron is 'old nog' or 'old cronk'. It's rather like a bittern but, of course, it's grey and not brown. Plenty of young shellduck around and no adults with them at all. They're either in Heligoland in the south-east corner of the North Sea or in Bridgewater Bay. They've left all the young ones behind to fend for themselves. Sometimes they leave an aunty behind to look after them but often they're left to their own devices. You just have to hope that crows or even a heron don't come marauding amongst them. Some mallard around of course – just coming out of their summer plumage and turning a rather dull brown colour. They're just coming back into their flight period again so, in the winter, we'll see them with bright bottle-green heads and plenty of variety of colour. You seldom come to this place without seeing something exciting. Today there's an egret. Normally you see them in the Mediterranean – in Portugal and Spain and further South too. We've had southerly winds so this one seems to have been blown off course and come all the way up here from Iberia. It's lovely. Pure white. Stalking through the shallows looking for food. A beautiful and graceful bird – and a real treat to see.'

The Alvis heads south-west past Dell Quay, through Birdham and on towards the Witterings. It is a calm, late summer day and the air is warm enough for the top to be down. After half-an-hour it comes to a halt at East Head. This is the mouth of Chichester Harbour and behind the sand dunes the tall masts of expensive yachts move backwards and forwards just breaking the skyline. Wearing sandals and tan shorts Richard Williamson strides towards the sea, his binoculars swinging round his neck: 'I've been visiting Chichester Harbour for more than a quarter of a century now. It hasn't changed as much as you'd think in that time. I come back each year to see all the same plants, particularly here at East Head. This has been a very dry year. The sun has been hot and it's been wonderful weather for looking at the dunes and the light on the mudflats and all the flowers blooming. They don't wither in a drought because the sand has a sponge of fresh water near the top of it held there by the salt water underneath. There are plenty of quiet nooks to find and to enjoy because the whole harbour shoreline is something like thirty miles long and there are perhaps three thousand acres of mudflats. Down at the harbour entrance there are ninety species of plants. You wouldn't believe it just looking around and I suppose with a quick scan you'd see only four or five. But once you get down on your hands and knees you start to find the tiny ones and they are very special to the dunes and to the salt marsh. They will grow nowhere else. This is why Chichester Harbour is regarded as a place of international importance not just for its birds but for its plants as well. There aren't many places like this left which are completely unspoiled. A lot of salt marsh has been built over and destroyed or reclaimed and is back to farm land – like the Wash on the East Anglian coast. For me this is one of the best sites in the south. There's masses of sea lavender here, great beds of it which cover the sand with colour. Equally beautiful to me though, is a quite rare little plant called sea holly. It's not related to the holly tree with its Christmas berries. It's a kind of thistle with lovely, small blue flowers. There's one particular plant of it on the dunes which I've known for twenty-five years. It's probably been here a lot longer than that though and it echoes the colour of the sea on a cloudless day. Another of my favourites is sea rocket, which always seems to colonise places like this. It's one of the first plants to start a dune going. It's able to exist in almost desert conditions. Sweet lilac-coloured flowers and fleshy leaves, which stop it from drying out. It holds its water in the stems. But it doesn't last long like the sea holly. It soon fades out when the dunes start to grow bigger. It likes its toes in the tide. What is amazing to me standing here today is what has happened here in the last quarter of a century. I remember in 1964 a great gale came along and blew all these sand dunes away. The tide washed them out into the saltings. Since then the National Trust has built them all back again. They planted sea marram grass to stabilise the dunes. And gradually, over the years,

Bearded Richard Williamson, Reserve Warden for the Nature Conservation Council at Kingley Vale with Chris Tyas, RSPB Warden at Langstone Harbour, among the reed beds at Fishbourne, home to many water birds.

all the plants have come back in, which gives me the chance to come out and enjoy them once again.'

It is not simple to gain access to every part of Chichester Harbour. Thorney Island, for instance, belongs to the Ministry of Defence. Though it is flat and featureless, it is also a fine place for watching the brent geese, which descend here in their thousands in the winter. But you have to get permission from the Military and to travel through manned barriers past gun-toting soldiers. Alternatively there is a long and arduous public footpath along its foreshore, which seems to make useless all the security on the main approach. Other prime spots are also difficult to reach especially in an old Alvis: 'Pilsey Island is right in the middle of Chichester Harbour. It's a small, sandy place and a nature reserve run by the Royal Society for the Protection of Birds. It's the best place in the harbour to see water birds in the winter time. As soon as the mud flats are flooded they fly in here and settle and gossip – talk about what's happening in their lives I suppose. You can get twenty thousand sometimes in the winter. But it's a hard place to reach. You have to come several miles along a footpath to get here. In the summertime things are fairly quiet. But some birds start to come in from about June onwards. By late summer or early autumn there are some small flocks around. You can get three or four hundred oyster catchers for example, which have just come down from Scotland and the Faroe Islands, where they've been breeding. Another bird to look out for is the tern. Some of them are here. They're becoming quite uncommon in Britain and the island gives them extra protection from predators, including human beings, some of whom want to collect their eggs. I've seen common terms, little terns and also a sandwich tern this year. But we're not always that lucky. One of the little terns has got chicks. They look like round pebbles rolled by the sea with brown and black markings on them. If they keep dead still in the shingle, you can't see them. The old name for the little tern is the sea swallow because of the long, white tail streamers which it's got. It's a delicate, streamlined bird seen against the blue of the water. It's pure white except for the black cap on its head, its yellow beak and short, stubby, yellow legs. It has graceful, long wings. In about a couple of weeks it will be setting out south on its big journey back down to the West coast of Africa. The parents of the chicks won't be going yet though. It's late to see them in August. Normally they hatch out in June. So this may be a second brood. Just imagine how vulnerable they would be if a crow or a magpie saw them. Think what a prowling fox at night would make of them, or even a tawny owl, which would gladly swoop down to take one. They're really very lucky to be able to grow up in the comparative safety of this nature reserve. There are ringed plover here too – often up to a thousand of them. They've got bold markings – white and black and brown, which give their faces a grumpy look. When they stand still they too look just like a big pebble. An old name for them was sand lark and another one, in the last century, was dull willy. It's a nice name but a little bit unkind perhaps.

Dunlin is the commonest wader here. In the winter you'll get twenty thousand sometimes. Their numbers have been gradually dwindling over the years. I don't know why and I'm not sure that anybody else does. They're small and they breed in Scotland and Iceland, in the Arctic tundra and lapland. They start to drift down here in the autumn. The wild fowlers of long ago, who shot everything they saw, called them ox birds. Another old name for them was plover's page because they would look small when they were flying in flocks beside some of the larger plovers – the peewits, grey plovers and oyster catchers.

The oyster catchers themselves are from various stations north and they've come to spend the winter in Chichester Harbour. Or it may be that they are on their way even further south, stopping off just for a week or two or maybe even a couple of hours before taking off and flying on south down to Spain and Portugal and the Mediterranean. Amongst them on the shore are black-tailed godwits with their long beaks. They look a bit like Concorde in flight. The big droop snout sticking out in front like the curlew but curved slightly upwards. Its enormous length gives them the great advantage of being able to probe deep into mud for the millions of tiny crustaceans and worms that live there.'

84

Most people who visit Chichester Harbour regard it as a place for small boats. There are nine thousand of them and, in the high summer, the waters are often crawling with them. They head down the harbour on the tide and most of them return as it ebbs. From the shore hundreds of waders and water fowl seem like spectators watching the human animals at play. There is naturally some conflict between people and their pleasures and wildlife. As man becomes slowly less stupid about these things, it is possible that he will begin to understand the need to care for and cherish the lives of creatures that are so much weaker and more vulnerable then he is.

DOWN the coast westwards the pressures on Langstone Harbour are even greater. Yet there is just as much worth preserving. The problem here is more industrial than recreational, though both play their part. Added to both are the scars which developers have left round the margin and which they continue to create today. Richard Williamson's father, Henry Williamson who wrote 'Tarka the Otter', came here in 1905 as a nine year old child and described it later in another book called 'Donkey Boy':

'. . . Now it was time to go away for the summer holidays . . . They were going to the seaside, to a faraway place called Hayling Island. The train went over the sea and they saw ships and boats and seagulls . . . At low tide the harbour was all mud and many of the boats lying there were old hulks and would never go to sea again, being abandoned. . . . Then after crossing the black bridge they were on Hayling Island passing cornfields and haystacks. And far away could be seen the Isle of Wight. The sea, the sea! There beyond gorse and brambles among patches of brown shingle could be seen a blue-grey placid level . . . It was a wonderful place with fishing boats, anchors, bathing tents, a lifesaving apparatus, a real lifeboat and porpoises coming up black out of the waves quite near the shore.'

You would have to be lucky indeed to find a porpoise in Langstone Harbour today. Much water, sewage and industrial waste have flowed in and out of its narrow entrance since those far-off days. People in their thousands still come here for a holiday by the sea. There are entertainments galore and many more diversions and eating places than there were at the turn of the century. Miraculously too there are still significant numbers of birds in the estuary, but in the main, the visitors seem unaware of them and of their beauty. Nor do they appear to spend much time admiring the magnificent colours in the sky or on the mudflats. The glitter of the Ferris wheel and the challenge of the one-armed bandit seem to satisfy their needs. For Richard Williamson, though, this is still a place to cherish and enjoy for the best of reasons: 'One thing that's vanished since my father's day is the old railway line. It was called the Hayling Billy Line and it was the last lap on his journey to the sea. It's now a footpath and from it you can watch much of the wildlife and the natural history of Langstone Harbour. It's quite sheltered and a pleasant, grassy path. In the gaps between the brambles you can see the birds and get quite close to them without frightening them. A white throated warbler greedily eats the early blackberries. It's going at them so hard because it needs to put on the five grams of fat which will take it all the way down to Africa when it migrates at the end of September. If ever you see a bird perched on top of a post out in the countryside and all by itself, ten to one it's going to be a windchat. They're a mixture of brown and cream. They've got a distinctive, off-white eye stripe. They're excellently camouflaged. They're heading south too at this time of year, down to France for the winter and on into Africa as well perhaps. Another small bird you'll see from the path is the wheatear. It used to be called 'whitearse' because it's got a white patch on its tail. People thought it impolite to say whitearse – Victorians I should think – so they called it wheatear instead. The cock bird, in addition to its white rump and upper tail-feathers, has a blue-grey back and blackish wings. Of course, there's masses to see on the water as well. Shoveller ducks for instance, so named because they've got a beak rather like a shovel. Even though the drake is still moulting at this time of the year, it's already got a lot of the dark greens, the whites, the buff and orange colours. It must be one of the prettiest ducks there are. They're dabbling ducks. They have to upend themselves and then to paddle furiously to keep themselves in this odd position. They're digging away in the mud for worms and molluscs and anything else they can sieve through their enormous beaks. Close to them is a little grebe, also called the dabchick. Most ponds and lakes will have one. It's a tiny bird, which looks a bit like a powder-puff. It's almost non-existent tail is just a tuft of downy feathers. Years ago fowlers used to shoot them and use their skins as hats because they have very thick feathers and a greasy skin. The sportsmen found that this would keep the rain off for hours on end. If you're quiet and careful on your walk along the track of the old Hayling Billy Line you may be lucky enough to see a kingfisher. For me it's the most beautiful bird in Britain. In spite of that it has the most disgusting nesting habits of any bird I know. If ever you get near one of the nests I don't think you'd want to go back again. They really do stink. They're eating fish all the time. Then they regurgitate pellets of fish-scales and bones. After doing this they often have to dive back into the water just to wash off the slimy mess. It's a bonus to see one nowadays because they're not all that common – only about five thousand of them in Britain now. Just as in Chichester Harbour there are plenty of herons here too. Their plumage is brilliantly adapted to stalking prey in the water because the colour is silvery grey with little black lines, which look rather like tiny wavelets along the shore. The light reflects off this plumage and the fish don't see the heron creeping up on them. I've watched a four foot eel being taken by a heron and they will occasionally catch mammals like rats. But most of their work is involved with small fish of the shallows like dab and plaice and, of course, they don't turn up their long beaks at water insects and creatures like that.'

WARDEN for the Royal Society for the Protection of Birds of a large part of Langstone Harbour is Chris Tyas, who spends much of his time afloat touring the estuary and keeping an eye on everything that is happening on his waters. Richard Williamson and Chris meet at a jetty on the south-western tip of Hayling Island and set out for a day's bird-watching together. The sun is bright overhead. The sky is cloudless and fresh with the beginning of autumn. The first few brent geese, the advance guard of thousands which will follow them, are already coasting in nervously to land. Before long they will be bold and possessive of the harbour's waters and of the surrounding fields and meadows. While Chris drives the boat, Richard steadies his elbows on the cockpit and observes the passing scene. The water is choppy and makes it difficult for him to look easily through his binoculars: 'This harbour is like a beautiful picture. So many colours and patterns and such a perfect scenery. The trouble is that, round the edges, bits are being reclaimed all the time. That's terrible because this place is a masterpiece. What the developers are doing is like going into an art gallery and cutting bits off the corners of pictures. The whole thing is complete in itself and nothing should be added or subtracted except for the birds as they come and go. I must say though, Chris, out in the middle of the harbour here it really is a picture and the huge numbers of birds make it perfect. I've never seen so many here, I don't think, and that is encouraging.'

'September's a very good time of the year to come out looking at the birds in Langstone Harbour, 'cos the waders have reached their passage peak by now.'

They're migrating south are they?'

'That's right – on their way to North Africa and those parts. Further south too, some of them. And then, before too much longer, we'll get all the birds here from the north, which come down to winter with us.'

'Now that the tide's dropping, Chris, I suppose that some of the wading birds are going to leave their high tide spots and come down to the edge of the harbour.'

'That's right, Richard. About two and a half to four and a half hours after high tide they move down, usually in small parties. It's an excellent chance to have a close look at them. There's a bunch of oyster catchers on their way down already. They're lovely, black and white birds with long, probing beaks. We've got them at their peak at this time of year with about two thousand of them in residence. That sort of number would stay here right through the winter.'

'What impresses me, Chris, is that the birds down here seem to be rather tame and untroubled by us.'

'They are – provided that you keep a reasonable distance away and don't make unnecessary noise or commotion. You can get excellent sightings of them from the boat provided that you don't get too close. If you do, they will be disturbed and fly off. If that happens too often, they're going to go away altogether. There aren't many other good places for them to go, so it's an important part of my job to control the numbers of boats round the places where the birds feed and to try not to let them get into a position where they scare the wildlife so that we lose it permanently.'

Langstone Harbour is a rectangle of water about five thousand acres in area. The RSPB reserve is thirteen hundred and seventy acres plumb in the middle. It includes the prime places for birds – some small islands, which rise just above the surface of the water. When the tide is right thousands of waders and water birds congregate there. Chris, tall, lean and bespectacled, is enthusiastic about their value. 'There's some of the best salt-marsh in the south of England on these islands. It's becoming quite a rare commodity nowadays. A lot of it has been reclaimed. What's left carries a mass of plant life. The plants in themselves aren't particularly rare. It's simply the fact that the salt-marsh itself is a scarce habitat these days. We've lost a lot to marina developments and other coastal work, particularly in built-up areas like this one. Portsmouth is very close. There's five hundred thousand people within easy travelling distance of the harbour. That causes every sort of pollution. But people aren't going to disappear. They're going to have to learn to be a bit cleaner about the way they live. Their sewage and litter has an effect on the whole ecology of Langstone, particularly on the levels of algae that we're getting. Another obvious problem is recreation – the sheer volume of boat traffic using the estuary. The whole Solent has got round about thirty-two thousand yacht berths and moorings. It's said to be the largest pleasure sailing fleet in the world. So that's the kind of pressure we face. Compared to Chichester, Portsmouth and Southampton Water, we're relatively quiet. And obviously we'd rather it stays that way. One surprising thing to me is that people still bathe here. Yet I wouldn't go anywhere near the water to swim. It worries me enough being sprayed by it as we chunter along in the boat, never mind actually immersing myself in it.'

The small boat slides ashore onto a tiny island close to the northern shore of the harbour. The traffic on the coast road below Havant can be plainly heard. This is the only island in the harbour with trees growing on it. Once there was a farm-house here with cattle and sheep. The farmer had to row ashore to buy his supplies. Today any animals would spend most of their lives up to their knees in mud and water on the marshland. Drinking water would have to be ferried out to them too since the old dew-pond is dry. The two men wade carefully onto the shore, secure the boat and head off to the far side of the island where the bird-watching is at its best. They settle down on the shingle and look south through their binoculars. Richard Williamson is the first to get lucky: 'Look, over there. Greenshank I think. Aren't they elegant? The old name for them used to be the green-legged horseman because of their long legs and the way they move. What do you think they're feeding on, Chris?'

'The swift and smooth way they're moving means they're after small fish I should think. Anything up to about an inch and a half long they will take. They're very quick birds and snap them up easily. Other times they'll go for invertebrates. They're certainly much better looking than the redshanks.'

'More oyster-catchers beyond them now. I don't think I've ever seen so many. Aren't they gorgeous with their evening dress plumage? Just like a line of head waiters or an orchestra tuning up for a symphony concert. Sounds a bit like that too with them all piping away. It's that most evocative sound of the sea marshes. A spectacular display. There are some ringed plovers close beside them. They were once called stone-hatches because their eggs, for camouflage, looked just like pebbles on the beach. What are they feeding on Chris?'

'They're after small invertebrates, which live on the surface of the mud. They tend to use their eyes for feeding. They've got short beaks so they can't probe into the mud like some of the other birds. They run along, stop, look and run again for more. There are some dunlin too – just coming in. Some of them are showing a little bit of summer plumage – others just a shadow of grey on the back of their winter colours. They have this black belly in the summer. You can see the last few flecks of the black on some of them there. In the winter they become a much greyer, more drab bird. They're finding something to eat every two or three seconds. These mud-flats are very productive areas for them. Unlike the ringed plovers, the Dunlin have got long beaks, which they probe in and feel with rather than just using their eyes. Interesting too that the beak is quite flexible and can move from side to side. It may look stiff, but down at the tip it can move quite a bit. There's also a curlew sand-piper out there – a healthy juvenile. It's got a down-curved beak. Much more elegant than the dunlin, this fellow. They breed up in the high Arctic, in the same places as the brent geese and the little stints. The fact that we've got lots of young curlew, sand-pipers and little stints this year means that we're going to get plenty of young brent geese later on. They usually come in mid to late September and, by Christmas, the numbers should build up to around about eight thousand.'

'Black-tailed godwits, Chris. They bred until 1830 in Britain and then they were wiped out. Now there are big numbers back here in the winter. How many have you got?'

'There are round about a thousand birds here at the moment. It will stay at about that figure for most of the winter. These ones are from Iceland and they represent about twenty per cent of the breed which will be wintering in Britain. Quite an impressive number. There's some grey plovers too sharing the island with them. Some of them are still in their summer plumage. Beautiful creatures with black faces and breast and silvery backs. Very smart birds to look at. And when they raise their wings you can see the black patch underneath, which is a good way of identifying them in flight.'

'Turnstones too, living up to their name and turning pebbles over for a living. They'll be finding sound-hoppers and tiny shore insects underneath.'

'They're birds which tend to feed right through the period of the high tide. Very busy fellows. We've got about four hundred of them at this time of year. It's the peak time for migration for turnstones now. So we've got two populations of them here at the moment. We've got the ones from Northern Europe, which are on their way through to Africa. And we've got another batch, which is going to winter here, which comes over from Greenland and Canada.'

As Chris and Richard leave the island they pick up some of the debris left by the tide on the high water line. Most of it is plastic and indestructible. Chris spends a significant amount of his time clearing up litter and rubbish. The four hundred and fifty sackfuls which he gathers each year only make a small dent on the problem. A recent survey carried out by the RSPB covered a hundred and twenty-three estuaries around the coast of Britain. It found that eighty were under some kind of threat and that thirty were in imminent danger due to the presence and behaviour of human beings. These findings are disturbing but Richard Williamson can still find reasons to be hopeful: 'In spite of all the people that surround this place, it is still a paradise. It's a beautiful stretch of water. Let's keep it beautiful. Let's keep it a paradise. The problems are the quality of the water and the air and the activities of humans around the margin. My father always used to tell me that, out in space, the world looked like a bubble. It's surrounded by pure air and pure water. If that bubble is burst, it disappears and we vanish with it.'

BURWASH

THE splendour of Sussex has always attracted painters and poets. From the sea and the downs up through the woods and the Weald and on to the fine farming of corn and cattle, the county is one of unique beauty and fascination. Its people too have strong and stubborn streak, which W. Victor Cook described in his poem, written at Sidlesham in 1946:

'Some folks as comes to Sussex,
They rackons as they knows
A darn sight better what to do
Than silly folks like me and you
Could possibly suppose.

But them as comes to Sussex,
They mustn't push and shove,
For Sussex will be Sussex,
And Sussex won't be druv.

Mus Wilfrid came to Selsey,
Us heaved a stone at he,
Because he rackoned he could teach
Our Sussex fishers how to reach
The fishes in the sea.

But when he dwelt among us,
Us gave 'im land and love,
For Sussex will be Sussex,
And Sussex won't be druv.

All folks as comes to Sussex,
Must follow Sussex ways,
And when they've larned to know us well
There's no place else they'd wish to dwell
In all their blessed days.

There ant no place like Sussex,
Until you goes Above,
But Sussex will be Sussex,
And Sussex won't be druv.

On the eastern side of the county and not too far from the Kent border, the village of Burwash, known to the locals as 'Burrish', is still one of the prettiest places in Sussex. The Reverend John Coker Egerton was the vicar here during the last century. In his book 'Sussex Folk and Sussex Ways' he remembers one of the villagers telling him that when the Romans landed in Pevensey Bay, they had with them a dog called Bur. After marching north with the soldiers, the animal was so muddy from struggling through the Sussex clay that he couldn't travel any further. So they washed him. From then on the spot they chose for the bath was called Burwash.

More certain historically is the tradition that the village was once alive with smugglers. It was whispered that contraband was hidden in the graveyard tombs and secret doors and passage ways can still be found behind the innocent walls of the cottages. In the churchyard the smugglers' graves are marked by the skull and crossbones, a bewildering sight in consecrated ground.

It was to escape from the adoring crowds in Rottingdean that Rudyard Kipling came to Burwash in 1902. He bought Bateman's, an old ironmaster's house, and lived there for the next thirty-four years. It was here that he wrote his famous Smugglers' Song:

'Five and twenty ponies
Trotting through the dark —
Brandy for the Parson
Baccy for the Clerk;
Laces for a lady, letters for a spy,
So watch the wall my darling
While the gentlemen go by.'

BURWASH crowns the top of an east to west ridge between Heathfield and Hurst Green, a hundred and twenty feet above the rolling Sussex Weald. The sloping gardens on either side of the busy high street look out over magnificent views, which inspired not only Kipling in his time but other local artists today. Jim Smith in Burwash Weald not only works with wood, clay, iron and glass, but is skilled in a dozen other crafts besides: 'I came up to Burwash from Bexhill in 1914. So I've had time to get acclimatised. There isn't a better place than this I should say. You get mountain areas that are as beautiful but you have so much rain there. We have a stable climate. Then we live close to a wood with all that has to offer. I camped out in the woods as a boy and used to sleep out there most nights. So I grew up with the stuff. I'm partly wood myself by now. Right from my late school days I've been wood-carving. It's the most beautiful material to work with. Even the plainest piece, when it's polished up, shows the lovely grain. We've got a big variety of hardwoods up here. That's what I mostly use. I can't call what I produce works of art because I never consider myself an artist. I'm too critical of what I do. I can see all the faults so

Jim Smith is a skilled craftsman, working with equal excellence in wood, clay, iron and glass.

93

clearly. But I enjoy it and that's the reason I do it. I've seldom sold anything. I've given a few bits away to members of the family. But otherwise I've got it all at home and the house is full of it. So it doesn't earn me a living. To do that, when I first left school, I thought I'd help the family fortunes and I took a job as a garden boy. But my father had started working with cars and he insisted that I go into the family firm with him. So bit by bit we built up our garage, which we ran for fifty-one years. We didn't make a fortune in the end but we had a good life. My brother did the mechanical side and I managed the forecourt and hammered out the bodywork.'

When Jim was a lad he worked for the Kiplings. After Rudyard's death, he restored the water mill at the bottom of the garden at Bateman's. Today it is back in business grinding wheat, and Jim's wife, Edie, Dorothy Martin and Alf Case all help in running it. As Jim winnows the grain, the mill stream floods into the water-wheel and the old cogs gently engage. The fine stone-ground flour is produced in the same way as it has been since Domesday: 'Years ago, a local society started work on the mill. They put in a new floor because there was nothing at all on the ground level. Then the job petered out because there was nobody to do the more complicated woodwork. I started by keeping a photographic record. But, being me, it didn't stop at that. I've had my saw-bench down here and made all the teeth for the gears and the framework that holds them in place. The mill machinery isn't connected to the building at all, so it needs a heavy, oak frame to support the gears. Then I had to set the bed-stone into the framework and next mount the running-stones and somehow to get the whole thing to work. It was quite an operation. We were lucky too in the early days because we had a former professional miller working with us for about four years until he died. He was only a youngster – around sixty-five. And what I know about milling I learnt from him. It's gone ahead well since then. As a matter of fact we can't grind enough flour for the demand. We often work the mill more than once a week. But we have a water problem because the river doesn't go through the pond any more. It means we only get water from the spring and that's restricted. So we have to rely on a good rainfall to keep us in business. I'm eighty-one now and I feel sure we can keep the thing going. Even when I'm through they're bound to find someone. We had some young farmers in one night when we were grinding but I didn't manage to get any of them interested. That's what it needs though. Youngsters coming down Saturday afternoons to help out and to learn would make all the difference.'

The air is cloaked with white dust. The sound of the machinery would lull you into an untroubled sleep if there was not so much work to be done. The clean wheat passes between the relentless stones and the good flour emerges and is carefully packaged. Outside, the Weald basks in the September sunshine.

THE countryside and the trees around Burwash are green and healthy in spite of a long, dry summer. Behind Dairy Court Farm, the home of Ray and Sheila Barber, the meadows are grazed by an odd assortment of contented cows, bullocks, ponies, sheep and donkeys. The farm has become an animal rescue operation and Sheila knows each of them by name: 'It's certainly quite a collection. We've got forty-five cattle of various ages, three donkeys, six ponies, four shires and ten sheep. I suppose we're a bit foolish really – other farmers would certainly think so. Knowing what would happen to them, we just couldn't send them in for slaughter. The donkeys are a good example. We got them from the village. They were going to be destroyed because they'd lost their grazing. That was about eight or nine years ago now and they're still here. Plenty of people try to persuade us to get rid of them. Butchers come round after the cattle and sheep. And a farmer friend of ours in Burwash, he sends folk around to try and buy them because he thinks we're a bit nutty. But we couldn't let them go. It started a long time ago with a heifer we had. She was going to be taken away for slaughter because her mouth was wrong. It meant that she couldn't eat hay – just the more expensive stuff. Well, it was costing us such a lot to feed her on concentrates that we decided that she'd really have to go. When the lorry came for her she sensed what was going to happen. She shot out of the yard and she came down into the field. We rounded her up, terrified and trembling, and put her in the truck. Once she'd gone we decided that was that and we'd have no more of it.'

Ray and Sheila walk the meadows looking over their livestock. All graze in harmony together. They even seem to appreciate the spectacular views across the Weald. The sheep bunch up and feed in a small flock, their age-old instincts teaching them to stick together for safety: 'Most of the sheep came from the slaughterhouse as premature lambs. Their mothers had been sent in with broken legs or something else seriously wrong. Then, when they killed the ewe, they found the lamb. We took them in and reared them. We've got ten at the moment, and some of them are pretty ancient by now. We hope that they'll die naturally. But we certainly wouldn't let them suffer. If something's ill, we'll always have the vet straight away. If he says it's in pain or that something's badly wrong, then he shoots it. Fortunately, we don't get too many of those. Usually he just gives them a few injections and they're all right again. But, as old age creeps up, I suppose there may be more for him to see to. The shire horses were another departure. We bought three of them as foals for showing. The fourth one – the grey mare – she was going to be put down and sent for meat when we got her. She was in a terrible state. She's come on well though she still suffers from colic. It all involves quite a long working day for us. In the summer it's not so bad 'cause they're all out of doors. But the winter time can be very difficult. All the animals are in the sheds and we get up at about five. I come out at six when Ray goes off to work. I begin by cleaning out all the loose boxes, where the ponies and the donkeys live. Then I go into the yard and start on the big horses. Next the small pens where the old cows are. We can't put them in with the bullocks or they get knocked about. The main yard has to be cleaned and then they're all fed. Later, but not long afterwards, we start again. It just goes round and round. By the time Ray comes home at five we have to do more cleaning out and feeding. In the summer it's different because they're out on the grass. But we have to check them over at least twice a day to be sure they're not being plagued by flies, which can give them New Forest eye disease, and to look out for mastitis. All in all it means plenty of exercise for us and for the dog.'

In one of the meadows Sheila gently holds the head of a placid donkey while Ray carefully pares its hooves with a razor-sharp knife. They talk quietly to one another and to the donkey while they work: 'I'm a Yorkshireman and we came south twenty-three years ago because Sheila's family were Sussex people. Of course I miss my county. All Yorkshire people do. But there's not much wrong with the scenery here either. Course, it's a bit different in the winter. When you come down here and it's blowing a blizzard it's not so good – though the bad weather certainly can't compare with the North. As for the donkeys' feet, they have to be trimmed regularly. I do them twice a year and it should be more often than that really. Anyway, they get seen to when they come out in the spring and again when they're going back inside come the autumn. It's just like with finger nails really. They grow quite fast and, if you don't keep 'em trimmed, they start to curl up. Then the animals are forced back on their heels when they walk, which isn't very nice for them. If you keep 'em cut they can go forward on their toes and that keeps their legs and everything in better condition. We've got three to do – the mother and daughter and the little Jack donkey. He's the odd one out. But he arrived with the others when we took them on eight or nine years ago. They've been together ever since. They're never apart. The reason they're so affectionate is that they're always getting titbits. They've almost come to expect them, they're friendly little things even without the food. How could anyone hate a donkey? They're so inoffensive. They don't do anybody any harm.'

SUSSEX is prime shooting country. Come the autumn no pheasant will be able to show its head in safety. Essential to successful shooting are the gun dogs, which Trish Hales from Court Cottage, Burwash has been training for as long as she cares to remember. She needs a lot of love and much patience to teach her labradors to become obedient and controlled. Trish lives close to a busy road and the dogs must learn to listen for her every command in spite of the roar of the nearby traffic: 'The main aim in training gun dogs is to find the wounded game when you're out on a shoot – whether it's pheasant, duck or mixed. You train your retrievers to fetch anything that can't be picked up by hand, because there's nothing worse than leaving wounded game lying around. Our whole purpose out on a shoot is to leave the ground clear. The birds have to be picked up by dogs with soft mouths. They must bring them in completely unmarked. They must have wonderful noses to follow and track anything that's wounded. And they have to have top quality intelligence, so the more they live with you the better they are. There are few worse things to my mind than the person who says all gun dogs should live in a kennel. Gun dogs give you more and make your life much more worthwhile if you live with them and they live with you. They need discipline, of course. Lots of it. But plenty of love too. My dogs are always with me when I'm at home, except for the puppies at sleeping time when I put them out in the kennel. The rest of the time all the adult dogs are always with me. They come out in the car with me. They go shopping with me. They visit friends' houses for supper. They sit on my knee and watch the television. I have one that is addicted to Westerns and, especially when the horses gallop across the screen, she just ups and wants to join in. I have another one who can't bear a dog to appear on the screen and we have growls and snarls in the corner because it's a strange dog invading our home.'

Outside in a sunlit meadow half-a-dozen sleek, black labradors career around Trish's legs as she leads them from the house. On her command they sit, watch and wait. One of the younger dogs is being taught to retrieve. Trish throws a padded dummy into the long grass, and, while the others watch enviously, the youngster waits and, when the order is given, dashes in to fetch it. If it has any difficulty, one of the older and more experienced dogs is sent in to show how it should be done: 'There are some people who think that pheasant-shooting is cruel and just for those with a lot of money. But the truth is that there's a lot of small farmers and other quite ordinary folk who have to scrape the cash together to buy themselves a gun. They're just regular country people. There's some too with a lot of money who come out. And it's true that there are some shoots run for the wealthy. But round here we like small, friendly shoots with the local farmers. The pheasants we shoot are, to me, like a crop. They are reared like chickens or calves are reared. Then they're turned out and they have a wonderful life in the woods running and flying wild. When the shooting season comes, they either get shot or they escape. Now, if you kill fifty per cent of the birds that are put out of the covers, you reckon you've done a really good job. And you very seldom get fifty per cent. So over half of the birds that are reared are left in the wild. And I think this is a great asset to conservation, because if there was no shooting there would be no pheasants in the countryside. After a few years they would die out. I've been doing this job with dogs and pheasants nearly since I got married. It was three years after my husband got back from the War and he had spent part of his gratuity money on buying a black labrador bitch. We've followed this blood line right the way through and the puppy which I'm training at the moment is a direct descendant from that bitch bought in 1945. She was a smashing old thing and we were very lucky to have started off with such a good one. Working labradors are much easier to train than pet bred ones, which have never been taught. They want to please and they expect to be trained. They hope that you'll be a disciplinarian and they are perfectly prepared to do what you tell them as long as you're not too soft with them. By that I mean not too soft in training, because they need lots of love and attention when they're not being taught. They are loving dogs and wonderful companions and they make perfect pets. But, above all, they make superb working dogs.'

In the long grass of late summer the black dogs look like seals as they leap along, their rounded backs rising above the waving green sea. They clearly enjoy one another's company but not as much as they appreciate the presence of their mistress: 'I had one of my grandsons aged five out training them with me. I was telling him how the dogs had to sit still and wait while you threw a ball or a dummy for them to retrieve. How each of them must stay until you told him to go and fetch it. One day I came into the garden and I found him with all the dogs tearing around after a ball. Everybody was crashing around and the boy was having a whale of a time. I just said gently: "Ian, don't you think it would be a good idea just to sit them up and to tell them to go one at a time?" "Oh no Granny", he replied, "that's not necessary now 'cos I've taught them to respond without command." For me though the real joy of training labradors is in all their funny quirks. It almost seems deliberate sometimes when they let you down at the most important moments. That's always when somebody who matters can see. Then, when they do something brilliant, there's never anyone there to appreciate it.'

BEFORE supermarkets marched into our lives robbing us of personal service and persuading us to buy all sorts of things which we neither need nor want, there were thirty shops in the village of Burwash. Most of them were family businesses and a few, happily, survive today. Eddie Workman, who was born here, still runs the Greengrocer's and the nearby Florist's. As in all proper village shops, these are the centres for local news and gossip: 'My mother first started in the shop when she left school. She worked at it for a few years and then packed it in to have her babies. First though she asked her boss, Charlie Brown, if she could have first refusal on the place if ever he sold up. When he retired, my mother and father bought it. That was about forty years ago when I was four or five. My parents knew Kipling of course. I think most people round here knew him a bit because he did wander about in the village. He wasn't as bad as a lot of people reckoned, but it's true to say that he wasn't very well thought of in Burwash. One of the old village boys told me the other day that Kipling used to go into the newsagent and would stand in there reading all the newspapers, even though he had quite a selection down at Bateman's. After he'd read all he wanted to he'd toss sixpence on the counter and walk out without taking any with him. The sixpence would have paid for the lot, so it wasn't mean. It was just unusual. Although he wasn't popular, I think it was because of his wife more than him that they took against him. I was told another story by one of the old villagers who knew a chap that worked on the farm down at Bateman's. Well, he fell asleep in the hay barn one day. Mrs Kipling found him there and woke him up by prodding him with a stick. She tore him off a proper strip and he said, "Oh, I'm sorry madam. But I've been up all night. My wife's just had a baby – and I was so tired." Well, unusually for her, she apologised and gave him a pound, which must have been an awful lot of money then, and told him to go home and look after his

Eddie Workman runs the Village Shop at Burwash, a centre for news, friendship and information as well as daily commodities.

wife and baby. It wasn't until some time afterwards that she found out that he was a single man.'

The shop is quiet and welcoming. Everything that a reasonable person could want is on the shelves. The customers all know Eddie and one another. So the atmosphere is friendly and intimate. No likelihood here, you would think, of any drama or bad behaviour: 'You might suppose everything's calm and untroubled. And to some extent it is. But we do get some nutters in here. We had one old boy that was a bit of a shop-lifter. He's dead now, but everybody knew about him. It was difficult to know how to deal with it. He'd come in first thing in the morning with a list his wife had written for him – bananas, carrots, potatoes and so on – and we'd write down the prices, add it up and he would pay. Then we'd scribble 'paid' on the bottom and that was it. Well, one day he came in and did his shopping. When he came to pay he was careful that I couldn't see into his bag. So it was clear that he'd got something extra in there. Anyway, at last I managed to have a peep and there was a packet of beefburgers, which weren't included on his list. I carried on looking after him, all the time trying to think how to approach the subject. It was only a quarter to eight in the

99

morning and nobody else was about. So how could I accuse him of pinching these things without upsetting everybody and making a big hoo-ha about it. In the end I just wrote on the bottom of his list in big, bold letters – "One pound of beefburgers ninety-nine pence". He paid up without noticing and off he went. After he'd gone I saw another packet of those beefburgers in the fridge and realised that they were only seventy-five pence. So he'd been overcharged by me. But we heard no more and I don't think he ever pinched anything else. So I felt quite pleased with the way I coped with that. It's the same with the flowers. You manage to pick things up as you go along. You have to. I started working with bedding plants when I was very young and soon got to know the different sorts and varieties. So I had a good basis. It was later that I began finding out about arranging them and making them into bouquets. When you've got to do something for somebody you find a way. I once done up a wedding arrangement that was something we'd never tried before. My wife wasn't too keen on the idea in case we didn't satisfy the customer. But we had a go and I don't think we did too badly. It's surprising really, if the chips are down you jolly well get on with it.'

Eddie is as much a part of the backbone of Burwash now as the doctor, the vicar or the bobby on the beat would have been in the good old days. He knows the village inside out and is the source of much advice, information and wisdom – all based on long experience: 'I've lived here all my life. So I should know the place and the people. When I was a kid we used to play football against the Fire Station door. We used to belt the ball pretty hard and one day we broke a window in the Station. But all was not lost. We were worried enough to open the door through the broken pane, get inside, measure it up and cut a bit of glass to fit, and we were out again before anybody came along. It was more than a month before they found they'd had a break in. Another of the stories I like to tell is about the newspaper round because we had papers in the shop for about ten years. We'd had lots of trouble with the women's magazines. They often came to us a week late or even more. This had been going on for about a month and, instead of arriving on the Tuesday when they were due, they'd come instead on the next Monday. So one day when I walked up the garden path to deliver a paper to one of the cottages a big notice was stuck on the door – "I have not had a Woman yet this week." Afterwards I wished I'd had the nerve to write on the bottom – "Well, it is only Thursday." Village life has changed now – and the people with it. The pace has altered and the conditions. People used to send their children to get the shopping with a note saying, "I haven't sent Willy with any money today 'cos I had nothing smaller than a ten shilling note." Nowadays the kids come in with twenty pound notes or fifty pound notes and think nothing of it. They just trip in, slap it on the counter and treat it as normal. And the goods people want have changed as well. A few years ago nobody bought aubergines, courgettes or avocados but now they're in great demand. They say to me: "What, no aubergines today? What am I going to do?" What's happened is that people have been abroad, they've tasted these things and they want them when they come home.

Well, that's fair enough and we're here to supply what the customer wants. But I think some of those new things are badly overrated. I can put up with kiwi fruit just about but mangos and fruit like that I can do without. It's sad that more of what we sell isn't grown locally. It used to be a good tomato area this. But most of those smallholders have gone. So there's not much stuff grown within ten or fifteen miles. I still get quite a lot from over the border in Kent and that's always very good.'

A pony and trap draws up outside the shop and Eddie dashes outside snatching up a can of Coca-Cola as he goes. It is not for the lady driver, nor for the two smart terriers sitting in the back. It is for the horse, which sucks down the drink just as though it was making a fortune in a television commercial. Suitably refreshed it sets off again on its elegant journey down the High Street.

BURWASH village has always been proud of the fact that it has its own volunteer fire brigade and fire station. It has been manned by none but local men since the turn of the century when the engine was horse-drawn and home-made. Every Monday the men have a practice and the Rose and Crown Inn is conveniently near at hand if they need to use Tom, the barman, as the body to be rescued. Officer in charge of the unit is Gordon Farmer, who remembers his father going out on fire drill and doing exercises with the Home Guard during the war: 'It's almost been a family affair this. In addition to my Dad, my brother-in-law was in the brigade when I joined and my wife's two brothers as well. Three of the others in the team had their fathers in it. So it seems to get handed on down the generations. There are eleven of us available so, with everyone working in the village, we can quite easily raise the crew of six which is what we need. We get all sorts of jobs apart from fires. I've been up a tree to get a cat out. I've been down a well to rescue a dog. My very first job in the brigade was one of the most unusual ones. We were called out to put a lady back into bed. She was being given a blanket bath by the local nurse and she'd rolled down between the bed and the wardrobe. The nurse couldn't budge her so we were called out to unjam her and get her safely back to bed. It all creates a bit of excitement in the village – that's for sure. When the alarm goes you often see the men streaking across the forecourt here with no clothes on as they change into their uniforms. I can make it official that the first streaker was not seen at Lords or Twickenham but right here in Burwash. We do have a serious job to see to of course and we have drills for special things like road accidents with chemical or other dangerous loads, rescuing people from crashed cars and plenty of hose-pipe and ladder exercises too. The difficulty with practices is that it's never quite the same as the real thing. I can always visualise what I want the men to do and they carry it out well. But it's without smoke, heat and flames. And it's difficult sometimes to get it over to the crew what it's going to be like in the emergency conditions. It's not for want of studying it. As a boy I used to come out on a Monday night to watch my father and then my brother-in-law when they were drilling. I also used to get my push-bike out as soon as I heard the siren going. I tried to follow the appliance as fast as I could go, to see where they were heading and what they were doing. So you can see it's always been my ambition to be a fireman.'

RUDYARD Kipling loved to walk in the beautiful hills and fields around Burwash. Perhaps part of the reason for that was to escape from the strictures of a dominating wife. But it was also to exercise his body and his imagination. He dreamed he could see traces in the downs of scenes from the past, relics of battles lost and won and whole settlements that had vanished through time. He recalled them in 'Puck's Song':

'See you the dimpled track that runs
All hollow through the wheat?
O that was where they hauled the guns
That smote King Philip's fleet.

See you our pastures wide and lone
Where the red oxen browse?
O there was a city thronged and known
Ere London boasted a house.

And see you after the rain the
Trace of mound and ditch and wall
O that was a legion's camping place,
When Caesar sailed from Gaul.

And see you marks that show and fade
Like shadows on the downs?
O they are the lines that Flint Men made
To guard their wondrous towns.'

INDEX